Simple Knots & Basic Ropework

Simple Knots &
Basic Ropework

GEOFFREY BUDWORTH

SELECT
EDITIONS

Select Editions imprint specially produced for Selectabook Limited

© Anness Publishing Limited 2000., 2001

Produced by Anness Publishing Limited
Hermes House
88–89 Blackfriars Road
London SE1 8HA

Publisher Joanna Lorenz
Project Editor Helen Marsh
Designer Michael Morey
Picture Researcher John Bolt
Reader Kate Henderson
Production Controller Joanna King

3 5 7 9 10 8 6 4 2

Printed and bound in Singapore

Nautical ropes on page 16 supplied by Footrope Knots.
Synthetic rope on page 16 supplied by Marlow Ropes Ltd.

Caution

Do not use any of the knots, bends, hitches, etc. in this book for a purpose
that involves forseeable risk of loss, damage or injury without the appropriate training
and equipment. Cavers, climbers, rescue workers, wilderness or ocean-going
adventurers who wish to use a particular knot for those (or any other) activities
and pursuits are strongly advised to seek the advice of qualified practitioners first.
This book is intended only to be a safe and simple introduction to knot-tying.

Contents

INTRODUCTION

Knotting is an enjoyable pastime. Most people can learn to tie knots, and even the complete beginner can soon acquire an impressive repertoire of useful or merely decorative knots. Knot tying is as absorbing as reading a good book, and the end product is as satisfactory as a completed crossword or jigsaw puzzle – but with many more practical applications. Everyone ought to know a few knots; that is why the International Guild of Knot Tyers (IGKT), founded in 1982, is now a recognized educational charity. Nobody should be over-dependent upon safety pins and superglues, patent zips (zippers) and clips and other fastenings, when a suitable length of cord and the right combination of knots are cheaper, consume less of the planet's scarce energy resources, and often work better. Knot tying can also be great fun! There are several thousand individual knots and an almost infinite number of variations of some of them. In addition, new knots emerge every year from the fingers of innovative knot tyers to increase the existing numbers. Then there are the ornamental aspects: macramé; leather-braiding and whipmaking; Chinese decorative knotting; Japanese *kumihimo* and other elaborate braiding or plaiting techniques; traditional British corn dollies; tassels, tatting and crocheting. Magicians and escapologists practise knot and rope trickery. Mathematicians venture into three dimensions when they explore the abstruse topological field of knot theory. Knotting is a delightful pursuit, and with a little guidance the novice can soon become adept at many new techniques. This book does not aim to cover everything outlined above, but the 100 or so carefully chosen knots it contains will act as an invaluable introduction to the subject. Those who wish to learn a few basic knots for practical use will find this an essential handbook, and others who want to learn to tie more elaborate knots will be able to progress from this comprehensive introduction on to more challenging knot-tying techniques.

KEY TO KNOT USER GROUPS

Angling/Fishing

Boating/Sailing

Caving/Climbing

General Purpose

Outdoor Pursuits

Materials

Rope has been made by man since the Stone Age, utilising the materials that were available. European hunter-gatherers, 10,000 years ago, grew only one crop – flax – and that was for rope, not food; the ancient Egyptians and Persians made rope from papyrus and flax. Even a captive orang-utan is reported to have made a kind of rope from its bedding material and then swung from it.

It is no surprise that man has gone to such lengths to develop and enhance rope-making materials. Rope enabled humankind to probe the deepest caves and to seek fuel and ores in underground mines; to migrate over rugged terrain with pack animals; to capture, harness and ride other beasts; to sail and cross oceans in search of treasure, trade, conquest and colonization. Rope concentrated the efforts of the labour force that built the great Egyptian pyramids and created the blocks and tackles with which medieval European stone masons erected their Gothic cathedrals and castles.

VEGETABLE FIBRE CORDAGE

As we have seen, until this century, rope was made from the shredded, combed and graded fibres of plant stems such as flax and jute, or from the leaves of sisal and abaca (hemp). It was made from fibres attached to seeds (cotton), and from other vegetable materials as diverse as fibrous coconut shells (coir),

NATURAL ROPE

A lefthanded (or S-laid) cable consists of three righthanded (Z-laid) hawsers. Each of these ropes has three lefthanded (counterclockwise) strands made from numerous righthanded (clockwise) yarns, spun from vegetable fibres.

horse and camel (even human) hair, date palms, reeds, esparto grass, wool and silk.

Because of its origins in nature, such cordage is also referred to as natural fibre. These fibres were spun clockwise (or righthanded) to create long yarns. Several of these yarns were next twisted up anticlockwise (counterclockwise) into strands. Finally, three strands were laid up clockwise or righthanded which created a typical rope.

The incurably romantic – who wish that square-rigged sailing ships were still commonplace – regret the demise of these vegetable fibre ropes, with their evocative smells and every shade of gold and brown; but, with the emergence of synthetic (manmade) cordage, the shortcomings of natural fibre ropes became intolerable. They were comparatively weak, even when scaled up to enormous diameters. Unable to withstand

SYNTHETIC (MANMADE) ROPE

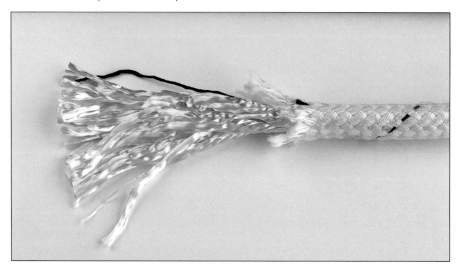

A 14 mm ($7/12$ in) diameter, soft matt polyester, 16-plait sheath encloses a hawser-laid core of several thousand high-tenacity polyester filaments.

◆ BELOW
Vegetable fibre knotted cordage in its natural element.

◆ BELOW
Natural fibre ropes vary in colour and may be blonde or brunette.

much abrasion, vegetable fibre cordage was also prey to mildew, rot, insects and vermin. It swelled when wet (so knots became impossible to untie) and froze in icy conditions with irreparable weakening as brittle fibres broke. Such ropes were also rough on the hands.

Obtainable only from specialized sources, and at a premium price, the use of natural fibre cordage is now very limited, – except in situations (such as filming a costume drama, rigging a classic wooden boat, and designing the interior decor and window dressing of nautical pubs, clubs and restaurants) where the appearance of an earlier period must be evoked. Some thoughtful

souls, however, concerned by what they perceive to be a profligate use of the earth's finite resources, prophesy an eventual return to natural fibre cordage, the raw materials of which can be harvested from renewable growing crops, without destructive ecological footprints.

Sisal rope is still sold for general purposes. Children shin up best-quality soft hemp ropes in school gyms. Coir is used for boat fenders. And for weather-resistant serving and seizing of wire and rope rigging by professional riggers, balls of tarred hemp spun yarn are still sold in several sizes.

It used to be that a rope could only be as long as the ropewalk (open field or long shed) where it

was made – although, of course, two or more could then be spliced together – but compact modern machinery has overcome this and, with extruded synthetic filaments, rope of practically any length can be made.

SYNTHETIC (MANMADE) CORDAGE

Discovered and developed by research chemists in the 1930s, the basic elements for synthetic cordage are: very fine continuous clusters of multifilaments, less than 50 microns/$\frac{1}{500}$ in across and of uniform diameter and circular cross-section; coarser monofilaments, individually more than 50 microns/$\frac{1}{500}$ in in diameter; discontinuous staple fibres (from

◆ LEFT
Sisal fibres are rough and hairy, but soft to
the touch.

◆ BELOW
Cordage lengths are no longer limited by
the extent of the ropewalk, either field or
long shed, where it was made.

Terylene and Dacron); poly-propylene, which is best for mundane domestic use; polyethylene (or Polythene), often sold as balls of twine; and a few so-called "miracle fibres" (such as Kevlar, Dyneema or Spectra) representing the latest and more expensive cutting edge of ropemaking technology. There are two grades of nylon: Nylon 66, discovered in the Du Pont laboratories, was the first manmade fibre of merit available to the cordage industry, and Nylon 6, subsequently developed by I.G. Farbenindustrie. Terylene was a British development from investigations at the Calico Printers Association, the sole rights were then taken up by Imperial Chemical Industries.

2 cm/⅝ in to 2 m/2 yd in length) made by cutting multifilaments or monofilaments into discrete lengths; and flat, narrow, ribbon-like strings produced from extruded split or fibrillated film. The brightly coloured balls of twine often found in hardware shops and stores are usually split film products, as are the larger balls and cops (cylindrical reels) sold at garden centres for horticulture use or as baling twines for agricultural machinery.

All of these raw materials make cordage that is size-for-size stronger and lighter than its vegetable fibre equivalent. A three-strand nylon rope is more than twice as strong as a manila one, yet it weighs half as much and may last four to five times as long. Many can be dyed a variety of colours (even including psychedelic patterns). Almost as strong when wet, they have a high tensile (breaking) strength and are also able to withstand sudden shock loading. Although not plagued by the ills that afflict natural fibre ropes, they are more susceptible to heat generated by friction – softening, melting and even parting in extreme cases.

The most common manmade materials are: polyamide (nylon), the strongest man-made cordage; polyester (best known trade names

◆ RIGHT
Man-made cordage is smoother than
natural yarn, but stronger.

MANMADE MATERIALS

"MIRACLE FIBRES"

Kevlar – discovered by Du Pont as long ago as 1965 – is an organic polymer immune to moisture and rot. Weight-for-weight it is twice as strong as nylon, but with low elasticity, and it has been used to replace wire halyards. Then there is Spectra or HMPE, the brand name of Allied Chemicals who manufactured this super-lightweight polyethylene (marketed by others as Dyneema and Admiral 2000). Its phenomenal tensile strength is greater than that of stainless steel. Released in 1985, it looks set to supersede Kevlar. The considerable cost of these will not deter ocean yacht racers or climbers, for whom competitive edge and extra safety margins are worth any price, but they are not recommended for routine knot tying.

POLYAMIDE (NYLON)

Polyamide is the strongest manmade cordage (although 10–15 per cent less when wet) and cheaper than polyester. It is very elastic, stretching under a load anything from 10 per cent to 40 per cent, then regaining its original length when the load is removed. This makes it suitable for mooring lines, also towing and rock-climbing ropes – but not in the restricted space of caves or crowded moorings, where stretchy ropes could be a liability. It does not float, so nylon can also be used for yachting anchor warps. The best colour to buy is white, as colouring may weaken the fibres by 10 per cent (while

certainly adding a lot to the price). A fairly high melting point of up to 260°C (478°F) ensures a reduced risk of melting due to friction; but be warned, it will, like all synthetics, soften and be irredeemably weakened at a much lower temperature than its melting point. Polyamide withstands attack from alkalis (and acids, to a lesser degree), oils and organic solvents. It has acceptable resistance to photochemical degradation from the ultra-violet wavelengths in sunlight, and to abrasion. Domestic consumers of this product will be impressed to learn that it is recommended for deep-sea towing and widely used in the off-shore oil industry.

POLYESTER (TERYLENE, DACRON)

Three-quarters the strength of nylon (but equally strong wet or dry), polyester does not stretch half as much, and pre-stretching during manufacture can remove most of the latent elasticity it does possess. Consequently it is recommended for standing rigging, sheets and halyards, where stretch is unwanted but high tensile strength is required, even replacing wire. It resists acids (and alkalis, to a lesser extent), oils and organic solvents. Like nylon, it does not float and it has about the same melting point and resistance to sunlight – but polyester wears better.

POLYETHYLENE (POLYTHENE)

Cheap, light (but it barely floats in water), without much stretch,

polyethylene is fairly hard-wearing and durable but has the lowest melting point of the four "poly" materials. It is sold in hardware stores as balls of twine and is used in the fishing industry, but it is too stiff and springy for most knot tying.

POLYPROPYLENE

In terms of cost and performance, this cordage may be ranked between vegetable fibre and the superior (nylon, terylene) manmade fibre cordage. Made from multifilament, monofilament, staple fibre or split film, it is the most versatile of synthetic fibres. Large quantities are manufactured and sold, at reasonable prices, via hardware and DIY shops and stores for all kinds of mundane work entailing no high performance risks. It has one-third to half the breaking strength of nylon and a much lower melting point – around 150°C (302°F) – rendering it useless for any task where friction generates anything approaching that amount of heat, but, as it is the lightest of the synthetics, and floats indefinitely, it is the obvious choice for lifelines and water-skiing towlines. It is completely rot-proof and resistant to most acids, alkalis and oils, but affected adversely by bleaching agents and some industrial solvents, while some cheaper brands denature in bright sun. For lovers of traditional cordage, there is a light brown rope – reliable, hardwearing and inexpensive – made from polypropylene to resemble hemp.

Types of Rope

Vegetable fibres are short and must be spun and twisted to create the long yarns and strands needed for rope. It is the countless fibre ends that give traditional ropes their characteristic hairy appearance and useful surface grip. Long synthetic filaments run the full length of the ropes they form, so manmade cordage is smooth – unless the filaments are purposely chopped into shorter lengths of staple fibres to make ropes that recapture the desirable handling qualities of the older natural cordage. More fibres and yarns make thicker cordage, and a rope that is twice the diameter of another will, as a general rule, be four times as strong (because the cross-sectional area has been quadrupled).

LAID

It is the twist and counter-twist imparted during manufacture that holds rope strands together and gives them their geometry, strength and flexibility. If very little tension is applied during the ropemaking process, the product will be floppy and flexible (soft laid), whereas great tension produces stiff (hard laid) stuff. Hard laid lines wear better but soft laid ones are preferable for tying knots. A three-strand rope is known as a hawser (and so is hawser-laid). Three hawsers laid up lefthanded make a nine-strand cable. Four-strand (shroud-laid) rope is less common and requires a core of yarns to fill the hollow space that inevitably occurs at the heart of such ropes. Lefthanded hawsers (and righthanded cables) are rare but not unknown. Textile workers, weavers and braiders prefer the terms S-laid (lefthanded) and Z-laid (righthanded) for the alternating twist and countertwist of yarns, strands and ropes.

BRAIDED

Braided vegetable fibre cordage has always been rare, except in small sizes for flag halyards and sash window cord. In synthetics it is commonplace and in many ways preferable to strands. An 8- or 16-plait (braid) is more flexible and stretches less than laid line. It does not kink, nor does it impart a spinning motion when loaded (as laid lines tend to do). Some braided cordage is hollow. In most, however, a separate core provides strength, elasticity and other essential properties, reinforced by the sheath, which adds extra surface characteristics, such as friction, feel, resistance to abrasion, sunlight and chemicals. This core may take several different forms, in which a braided outer sheath encloses heart strands that can be braided, laid or composed of parallel multifilaments, monofilaments or yarns. Braid-on-braid is acknowledged to be the strongest of cordage constructions and braided synthetic lines are the most versatile of all cordage.

PLAITED

Eight or sixteen ropes, usually nylon, are woven in pairs to create mighty mooring warps for supertankers.

SHEATH-AND-CORE

Climbing ropes are a special class of cordage, often referred to by the European designation kernmantel (core-sheath). Static ropes take the full weight of climbers and are designed for the wear, tear and occasional short fall of regular climbing; while dynamic ropes are used for safety, generally unloaded, but with the extra elasticity and integral strength to cope with potentially disastrous falls and uncontrolled spins. Single ropes are manufactured in 11 mm/⅖ in diameters, plus or minus 5 mm/ ¼ in, while half-ropes of 9 mm/ ⅜ in diameter, plus or minus 2 mm/1/12 in, are intended to be used doubled. Climbing ropes should have high melting points to absorb the heat generated by abseiling (rappelling) and belaying. Obtain specialist advice on the detailed properties of these ropes and look for the UIAA (Union Internationale des Associations d'Alpinisme) label of approval.

Kernmantel accessory cord, used for slings and other attachments, can be obtained in diameters that range from 4–11 mm/⅙–⅖ in.

Woven nylon webbing comes in widths from 10–75 mm/5/12–3 in, but the width most commonly seen is 25 mm/1 in. A tubular tape, resembling a flattened hollow tube, handles and knots easily due to its suppleness, but a flat weave, similar to that found in car seat belts, is stronger, stiffer and has better resistance to wear and abrasion. It is highly versatile and not too expensive for harnesses, belts and slings, and it also makes excellent luggage rack lashings (straps) for cars and vans.

	KEY TO TYPES OF ROPE
1	8-strand nylon, 16 mm/⅔ in anchor braid.
2	3-strand nylon, 14 mm/7/12 in hawser.
3	3-strand polyester, 14 mm/7/12 in hawser.
4	3-strand spun polyester, 14 mm/7/12 in hawser (resembling natural fibre rope).
5	3-strand monofilament polypropylene, 14 mm/7/12 in hawser.
6	3-strand staple/spun polypropylene, 14 mm/7/12 in hawser.
7	16-plait matt polyester, 14 mm/7/12 in braid-on-braid rope, with an unusual core (itself a 16-plait enclosing an 8-plait), creating three concentric layers.
8	16-plait matt polyester, 16 mm/⅔ in braid-on-braid rope (with a double layered core, as above).
9	16-plait pre-stretched polyester, 16 mm/⅔ in braid-on-braid (with an 8-plait core) rope.
10	16-plait Dyneema, 12 mm/½ in braid-on-braid rope (with a two-layered core).
11	16-plait Dyneema, 10 mm/ 5/12 in braid-on-braid rope (with a two-layered core).
12	16-plait polypropylene, 9 mm/ ⅜ in braid-on-braid cord (with a hard-laid 8-plaid cord core).
13	16-plait polyester, 6 mm/¼ in sheath-and-core cord (with a heart of four 3-strand strings).
14	8-plait matt polyester, 10 mm/ 5/12 in braid-on-braid rope (with an 8-plait core).
15	8-plait multifilament polypropylene, 8 mm/⅓ in braid-on-braid cord (with an 8-plait core).
16	8-plait pre-stretched polyester, 6 mm/¼ in sheath-and-core cord (with a heart of three 3-strand strings).

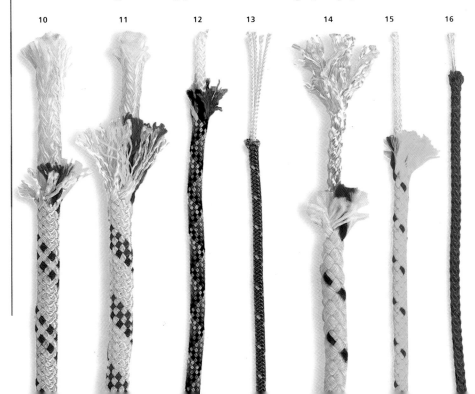

10   11   12   13   14   15   16

Breaking Strengths

Ropemakers' brochures and leaflets usually contain tables listing the minimum average breaking load of every type and size of their cordage products. Unfortunately, the data differs from company to company, depending upon the tests and equipment each firm uses, making comparisons difficult.

SPECIFICATIONS

Product specifications may blur the facts: for example, a "mooring line", made for specialized markets, may consist of an elastic nylon core inside a hard-wearing polyester sheath, while many mass-produced and comparatively cheap cordage items, sold for the domestic market, can be much weaker. Nevertheless, an appreciation of the main rope and cordage species can be gained from the following outline. The minimum breaking strength of a 4 mm/⅙ in diameter slim nylon cord of 3-strand or 8-plait construction is likely to be around 320 kg/705 lb, which might withstand two 159-kg/25-stone Japanese sumo wrestlers having a tug-of-war. For standard 3-strand polyester of the same diameter the figure is a trifle lower – 295 kg/650 lb – but an 8-plait construction combined with pre-stretch treatment changes that to around 450 kg/990 lb. Polypropylene of the same diameter is variously quoted at 140 kg/309 lb, 250 kg/551 lb and even 430 kg/925 lb; polyethylene is about 185 kg/408 lb, while the average breaking strength of a 4 mm/⅙ in cord of Dyneema/Admiral 2000/Spectra is a remarkable 650 kg/1,432 lb. To achieve these kinds of performance with natural fibres, it would be necessary to have at least a 25 per cent increase in diameter to 5 mm/⅕ in manila or 33.3 per cent to 6 mm/¼ in sisal.

LARGER SIZES

With a 10 mm/5/12 in thin nylon 3-strand hawser, the minimum breaking strength increases to around 2,400 kg/5,292 lb. That is almost two-and-a-half metric tonnes, the weight of a large motor vehicle. Again, the average figure is somewhat less for polyester at 2,120 kg/about 2 tons; 1,382 kg/1⅓ tons for polypropylene; and 1,090 kg/just over a ton for polyethelene. Dyneema/Admiral 2000/Spectra, by contrast, would be about 4,000 kg/about 4 tons. The same size of rope in manila could only cope with 710 kg/1,565 lb and sisal with 635 kg/1,400 lb.

Finally, for a sizeable 24 mm/1 in rope diameter, the average quoted breaking strengths are: nylon = 13 tonnes/12.8 tons; polyester = 10 tonnes/9.8 tons; polypropylene = 8 tonnes/7.9 tons; polyethylene = 6 tonnes/5.9 tons; and Dyneema/Admiral 2000/Spectra = a stupendous 20 tonnes/19.7 tons. Even the best manila would have to be nearly twice that size (and four times as strong) to match those figures.

✦ LEFT
Vegetable fibre cordage is much weaker and generally has a shorter life than synthetic products.

Synthetic cordage is much stronger and generally has a longer life than products made from vegetable fibre.

COMPARING AND CONTRASTING NATURAL FIBRE AND SYNTHETIC FIBRE ROPES

	NATURAL FIBRES				SYNTHETIC FIBRES			
	Sisal	Cotton	Hemp	Manilla	Polyethylene	Polypropylene	Polyester	Polyamide
Shock loading	●	●	●●●	●●	●	●●●	●●	●●●●
Handling	●	●●●●	●●●	●●	●●●	●●●	●●●●	●●●●
Durability	●	●●	●●●●	●●●	●●	●●●	●●●●	●●●●
Rot & mildew resistance	●	●	●	●	●●●●	●●●●	●●●●	●●●●
U.V. resistance	●●●●	●●●●	●●●●	●●●●	●●	●	●●●●	●●
Acid resistance	●	●	●	●	●●●●	●●●●	●●●●	●●●
Alkali resistance	●●	●●	●●	●●	●●●●	●●●●	●●●●	●●●●
Abrasion resistance	●●	●●	●●●	●●●	●●	●●	●●●●	●●●●
Storage	dry	dry	dry	dry	wet or dry	wet or dry	wet or dry	wet or dry
Buoyancy	sinks	sinks	sinks	sinks	floats (just)	floats	sinks	sinks
Melting point*	not affected	not affected	not affected	not affected	about 128°C (about 262°F)	about 150°C (about 302°F)	about 245°C (about 473°F)	about 250°C (about 482°F)

Key: ● poor ●● acceptable ●●● good ●●●● excellent
* Note that cordage softens and weakens at perhaps 20–30 per cent lower temperatures.

SUMMARY

These data take no account of fair wear and tear (including knots), damage or misuse (e.g. shock loading, or excessive friction). Consequently a safe working load will be considerably less – perhaps a fifth to a seventh of the quoted strengths. Then again, it is often necessary to buy synthetic cordage many times stronger than actually required; for example, a 4 mm/⅙ in cord would not match a block and tackle made for 25 mm/1 in rope even though it might be able to cope with the intended load, nor could it be comfortably grasped in the hand and heaved.

Knot tyers do not normally need to know either the molecular structure of cordage or its test data interpreted in charts and graphs. Cavers and climbers, flyers (of gliders and microlight aircraft), and all who calculatingly engage in potentially hazardous pursuits – from astronautics to undersea exploration – can obtain these technical details from the manufacturers. For the average user, a general knowledge of the main types of cordage is all that is needed to buy shrewdly and sensibly.

Care of Cordage

Do not leave rope or smaller stuff (cotton, thread or string) exposed needlessly to bright sunlight. Avoid any chemical contamination (for example, car battery acid). Protect synthetics from heat-generating friction, spark-spitting camp-fires or acetylene-cutting torches, and all other kinds of combustion. Try to avoid letting wet rope freeze. Store cordage in a dark, dry and cool place with good air circulation; relative humidity should be 40–60 per cent and the temperature 10–20°C (50–70°F). Wash dirty ropes in warm water to remove abrasive grit from their fibres and then dry them gently; similarly, at the end of a sailing season, soak and rinse in fresh water ropes that have been exposed to salt crystals. Abrasion can result from careless

♦ ABOVE
WRAPPED & REEF KNOTTED COIL
Rope and smaller cordage alike may be transported this way, in a bag or the boot (trunk) of a motor vehicle, with a realistic hope that it may be retrieved tangle-free at the end of the journey.

♦ LEFT
ALPINE COIL
Climbers favour this means of carrying their ropes.

handling in a rough environment or from ill-fitting blocks, cleats, or fairleads, but fair wear and tear is inevitable, whether it is from regular use or from being kept in the same position for prolonged periods. Even unused rope that has been carefully stored will age and become less reliable.

INSPECTING ROPES
Inspect ropes periodically, metre by metre/yard by yard in a good light, for loose, worn and broken surface yarns and cut strands. Some surface fluffing is inevitable; it is fairly harmless and might actually afford slight protection from further wear. Chemical attack can show as staining and

♦ BELOW
FIGURE-OF-EIGHT COIL
Storekeepers prefer this method, which
provides a loop for hanging ropes.

softening. Heat damage is harder
to identify, unless fusing and
glazing are detectable. Internal
wear and damage can be seen by
carefully opening laid strands but
may be concealed in braided stuff
(when the core could be weakened
while the sheath remains relatively
unworn and lacks obvious
damage).

So a risk assessment for braided
lines must also take into account
their recent history of use and
abuse. Worn-out rope looks its
age. It is often attenuated
(weakened by stretching), with a
reduced diameter and a more
acute angle of lay between the
strands. Sheath-and-core ropes
can develop creep, the sheath
moving separately from the heart
strands. Climbing ropes and those

♦ BELOW
FIREMAN'S COIL
Elegantly simple, this method deserves to
be better known.

used with lifting tackle must be
pensioned off long before they
reach such senescence. Each rope
should have its own log book in
which its working history is
recorded. Communal club ropes
(that anyone might use at any
time) should be retired after two
or three years, but individually
owned and maintained ropes may
be used for four to five years,
then down-graded for teaching
knots and other points of general
use that do not involve climbing.

It has been observed that rope
with a mind of its own, awkward
to manipulate and a trifle
disobedient, is generally at the
height of its powers. By contrast,
rope that is soft and amenable, a
pleasure to handle, should be
condemned and discarded. There
is some truth in this. Do not tread
on rope, allow it to be nipped or
become kinked, or drop it from a
height. Coil ropes loosely and
then hang them up on pegs well
above the floor.

Tools

◆ BELOW
Tying elaborate knots is made easier
with one or more handy tools (see key
to illustration).

Acquire a sharp and robust craft
knife to cut rope and cord;
scissors work only on thin strings
and twines. Most of the knots in
this book can be tied and
tightened with just the fingers,
aided now and then with a prod
from the pointed cap of a
ballpoint pen. A few of the
slightly trickier knots are more
easily completed with one or
more of the following tools.

GRIPFIDS

Handmade by rope craftsman
Stuart Grainger, these resemble
small Swedish fids, with the
refinement that the tip clings to
working strands, pulling them
through knotwork as the tool is
withdrawn. Two sizes cope with
cordage up to either 7 mm/³⁄₁₀ in
or 12 mm/½ in diameter.

NETTING NEEDLES

These serve as bobbins for storing
quantities of small cords tangle-
free and ready for immediate use.
Sizes range from a tiny 11.5 cm/
4½ in to jumbo-sized ones 30 cm/
12 in or more in length. Shun
crudely made ones in favour of
those that are polished to a
smooth finish. The seller will
show you how to load them.

ROUND-BILLED PLIERS

Handy for tightening knots with
lots of crossing points. Most high
street hardware shops or do-it-
yourself superstores will have
them. Choose a pair to suit the
scale of work: a small size
(sometimes called "jeweller's

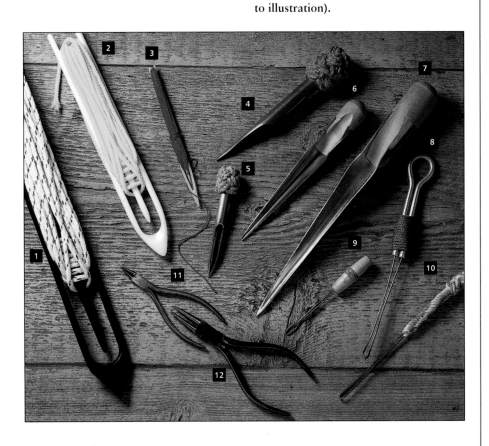

pliers") will have an overall
length of about 10 cm/4 in,
with more robust sizes from
about 15 cm/6 in upwards.

SWEDISH FIDS*

These are used to poke and prize
open gaps through which
working strands can be tucked
and pulled. Obtainable from
yacht chandlers and serious rope
stockists, they range in length
from about 15 cm/6 in to 38 cm/
15 in or more. Choose a size to
match the scale of your work.

WIRE LOOPS

Homemade from stiff and springy
wire 0.25 cm/¹⁄₁₀ in diameter – or
thinner – inserted securely into a
handle, these are indispensable
alternatives to fids when working
with smaller stuff.

KEY TO TOOLS	
1	Netting needle (large)
2	Netting needle (medium)
3	Netting needle (small)
4	Gripfid (large)
5	Gripfid (small)
6	Hollow "Swedish" fid (small)
7	Hollow "Swedish" fid (large)
8	Homemade wire loop (large)
9	Homemade wire loop (small)
10	Homemade wire loop (medium)
11	Jeweller's pliers
12	Round-billed pliers

* Originally fids were solid
hardwood spikes. They can
occasionally be found in antique
shops or markets as collectable
treen (lathe-turned wood).

Cutting & Securing Ends

TYING & TAPING

Before cutting any natural fibre cordage, first tape or tie it to prevent fraying. Adhesive tape is the least attractive option – and unacceptable on finished craftwork – but it is used a lot in preparatory stages as an easy alternative to whipping. Wrap where the cut is to be made and then simply slice the tape in half to achieve two bound ends at a stroke. Alternatively, tie a pair of strangle or constrictor knots, one on either side of where the cut is to be made.

HEATING & SEALING

This is now widely practised by ropeworkers and riggers. There is no need to tape or tie heat-sealed ends. Rope manufacturers and stockists have electrically heated guillotines to cut-and-seal the ropes and cords they sell. These cost too much for most of us, so the comparatively cool yellow flame of a struck match may have to do on small stuff. For large diameters, or to cut-and-seal a batch of strands, heat the blade of an old penknife in the blue flame of a blow-torch until the tip and edge glow cherry-red. Pause to re-heat it every few seconds for a clean and fast cut. Nylon melts, drips and burns with whitish smoke and a smell said to resemble fish or celery; it may even flash into a small flame (easily blown out). Polyester melts, drips and burns with dense black smoke and a smell like mushrooms. Polypropylene and

TYING

1 Tie two constrictor knots, one either side of where the cut will be made.

TAPING

1 Wrap a turn or two of adhesive tape around the rope or cord.

HEAT SEALING 1

With an electric guillotine or a heated knife blade (not shown), cordage and small diameter ropes may be neatly cut and sealed.

polyethylene react at lower temperatures, shrinking rapidly away from the source of heat. It is possible to pinch the soft heated ends to a point, rolling them between forefinger and thumb, before they harden, but take care

2 Slice vertically down halfway between the two binding knots already tied.

2 Cut vertically down through the middle of the taped portion.

HEAT SEALING 2

Use the naked flame of a match or cigarette lighter for a quick but often lumpy seal.

to wet the fingertips first or it may cause a burn and blister. A cord that appears to be synthetic but actually chars and even ignites without melting, is probably made from rayon, which comes from wood pulp.

Terms & Techniques

Anyone who ties a knot is described in knotting circles as a tyer (not tier) since the former is unambiguous while the latter has a different meaning when written.

SIMPLE TERMS

The end actively involved in the tying process is referred to as the **working end** or sometimes – by anglers – as the **tag end**; the in-active remainder is known as the **standing part** and **standing end**. Doubling a line so that two parts are brought close together creates a **bight**. If this is done to locate the exact centre of the bit of stuff in hand, then one is said to **middle** it. Once the two adjacent parts cross, a bight turns into a loop; a further twist creates a couple of **elbows**, while the process of turning a bight or loop into an improvised eye by wrapping the end several times around the standing part is referred to as **dogging**. Any loop that is pulled

so small that it deforms and damages a rope becomes a **kink**.

The word **rope** is generally defined as meaning any plaited, braided or laid (in strands) product over 10 mm ($5/12$ in) in diameter, although there are exceptions (for example, some

climbing ropes are 9 mm/⅜ in diameter). Anything much smaller is referred to as **cord**, **string**, **twine** or **thread**. Rope and cord are collectively called **cordage** but, more commonly, **stuff**. A rope or cord dedicated to a particular job becomes a **line** (tow line, washing line, lifeline, throwing or heaving line), or acquires an even more specific label (lanyard, lashing or lassoo). A lightweight throwing or heaving line that is used to haul a heavier line across an intervening space is known as a **messenger**. The terms **plait** and **braid** are virtually interchangeable. There are, however, some who say that braids are flat while plaits have a three-dimensional cross-section.

Ropeworkers often "take a **turn**" in order to check a load by means of the friction it applies. Wrapping the working end an extra amount to bring it alongside the standing part, so as to tie it off, produces a **round turn**. Converting a single-ply knot to two, three (or more) ply involves following the original **lead** of the knot around with the working end. The place within a knot where the collective friction of its parts is concentrated is known as the **nip**. The tuck that finally secures a knot, preventing it from collapsing or unravelling, is the **locking tuck**. A simple loop is an **overhand loop** when the working end lies on top of the standing part, becoming an **underhand loop** if the working end goes beneath the standing part.

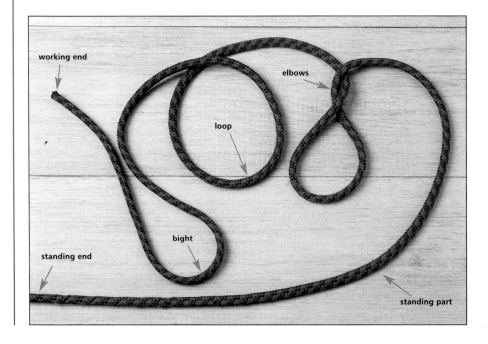

working end

elbows

loop

bight

standing end

standing part

1 More often than not, a clove hitch may have been tied with the working end.

2 But slide the knot sideways off its foundation – and it will fall apart.

3 Once separated from its foundation, nothing remains of the knot but the line in which it was tied.

4 To re-tie the clove hitch, this time in the bight, first cast an overhand loop.

5 Create a second underhand loop immediately alongside the first one.

6 Twist the loops to overlap them. The resulting clove hitch may be slid back on to its foundation.

TYING TECHNIQUES

Most knots can be tied in more than one way. The methods illustrated have been chosen either because they are easier to learn or to photograph clearly. Practised knot tyers develop more dextrous ways to tie knots that are almost sleight of hand. Discover these slicker and quicker tying tricks for yourself: with a completed knot in your hands, back-track, untying the knot a step at a time, to see how it is

created. A short cut may occur to you. Re-tie it that way in future.

Tying a knot "in the bight" means doing so without using the working end. When a hitch or a binding knot collapses to nothing if slid from the foundation around which it was tied or a loop knot can be unravelled without recourse to its ends (in other words, it "unties in the bight"), then it can be tied in the bight. This is the "law of hitch & bight" proposed by Harry Asher

in the mid-1980s. A surprising number of knots may be tied this way. Knowing the principle can also enable knot tyers to spot subtle differences in seemingly identical knots: for example, the bag knot can be tied in the bight but the miller's knot cannot.

Most knots must be drawn up gradually so as to remove slack and daylight before gently pulling on each end and standing part in turn to create a knot that remains snug and firm.

BASIC KNOTS, BENDS & HITCHES

All knotting may be summed up under three main headings: Knots, Bends and Hitches. A hitch attaches a line to a post, rail, spar, ring or even another rope. A bend joins two ropes together. A knot is anything other than a bend or a hitch (including stopper knots, binding knots and loop knots) although the word "knot" is also used, sometimes confusingly, in a general way to refer even to bends and hitches. These 12 basic knots are some of the easiest to tie; discover how simple yet versatile they can be. All you will need is two lengths of flexible cord, each 1–2 m/3–6½ ft long and from 5–10 mm/⅕–⁵⁄₁₂ in in diameter.

Simple, Overhand or Thumb Knot

This is the most elementary stopper knot, to prevent small stuff (cotton, thread or string) from fraying or pulling out of a hole through which it has been threaded. Its uses range from securing thread in a needle to tying loose change into the corner of a handkerchief when on the beach or anywhere else where deep pockets are temporarily not available. Nobody ever has to be taught to tie this knot. It just comes naturally.

1 Make an overhand loop in the small stuff that is to be tied.

2 Tuck the working end through the loop already formed and pull on the standing end to tighten the knot.

Overhand Knot with Drawloop

Drawloops act as quick releases, and may also strengthen some knots by bulking them up with an extra knot part. Overlooked and underrated by many knot tyers, drawloops deserve to be used more, and will from time to time be recommended in this book.

Start to tie a simple overhand knot but stop before the working end has been fully pulled through.

Two Strand Overhand Knot

This is another knot that the youngest person can tie instinctively. It creates a bigger stopper knot, for cottons or domestic string, and also acts to hold cords together as long as they lie in the same direction, for example, to prevent a waist tie in pyjamas, swimming trunks or tracksuit trousers (sweatpants) from pulling out when not in use. NB: This is not a bend because the two cords are not aligned to be pulled in opposite directions.

1 Place the two strings or cords to be tied parallel and together.

2 Tie a simple overhand knot. Tighten, taking care to keep the lines parallel (like railway tracks) throughout.

Double Overhand Knot

This forms a chunkier stopper knot than the simple overhand knot, although it will not block a larger hole. It is, however, an indispensable technique for other knots that are based upon it.

1 Tie an overhand knot – but tuck the working end a second time.

2 Gently pull both ends apart, at the same time twisting them in opposite directions. In the example shown, the lefthand thumb goes up and away from the tyer, the righthand thumb down and away. The cord dictates what it wants to do; simply go along with it. See how a diagonal knot part wraps itself around – let it happen. Pull on both ends at the same time to tighten this knot.

Overhand Bend

Also known as the tape knot, this knot is recommended for the flat or tubular woven webbing (tape) used by cavers and climbers – although it works in anything from the largest cables to the finest angling monofilaments.

2 Follow the lead of the original knot with the second working end.

1 Tie an overhand knot in the end of one of the two lines to be joined. Insert the end of the second line.

3 For a twofold knot, ensure that all knot parts are parallel and that the short ends emerge at the top of the knot as there is some evidence that it may be stronger this way. Pull the standing parts to tighten.

Fisherman's Knot

The reliable fisherman's knot can be used for anything and everything from domestic to heavy industrial tasks. This is a knot that can be untied if it has been made from rope, but if you make it out of string you will have to cut it off.

1 Lay the two lines parallel and close to one another, tying an overhand knot with one end around the standing part of the other.

2 Turn the half-completed knot end-for-end and tie an identical overhand knot with the other end. Pull first on both working ends to tighten the individual knots, then on the standing parts to unite and tighten the knot.

Single Hitch

Commonly referred to as a half hitch, alone this is an unreliable means of attachment except for the most temporary and trivial of purposes (when a drawloop might help) but it is the means of finishing off other more substantial working hitches.

1 Tie the ubiquitous overhand knot around something firm, such as a fat felt tip pen, to discover how this careful rearrangement traps the working end.

2 Leave a longer working end, which is not completely pulled through, for a drawloop.

Two Half Hitches

Two half hitches are the tried and trusted way to secure a line to a ring, rail or anything. They are always identical, i.e. the working end goes the same way around the standing part in both cases.

1 Tie a single half hitch with the working end of the line.

2 Add an identical second half hitch and draw them snugly together to complete this useful attachment.

27

Round Turn & Two Half Hitches

This is a classic hitch, comparatively strong and secure, the name of which describes it exactly. It can be used to secure a boat, to tow a broken-down vehicle or secure a load.

1 Take a turn around the anchorage, bring the working end alongside the standing part, and apply a half hitch.

2 Add an identical half hitch to complete this dependable knot.

Overhand Knot & Half Hitch

This loop knot has been used by weavers to rig looms, by Inuits (Eskimos) to string bows, by anglers as a leader loop for tackle, and for starting to tie parcels. It is sometimes called a packer's knot.

1 Tie an overhand knot with a large drawloop and adjust the loop to the required size.

2 Wrap and tuck a half hitch with the working end around the standing part. Tighten by pulling on each one of the loop legs in turn.

Double Figure-of-Eight Bend

This knot is similar in function to the fisherman's knot but, unlike that knot, it is bilaterally symmetrical (both sides look the same). Several knots with a figure-of-eight layout are referred to as Flemish knots, and an alternative name for this one is the Flemish bend. Leave the knots a few inches apart for a knot that will absorb a sudden jerk or snatch by sliding before it holds.

1 Tie a figure-of-eight knot in one of the two lines and insert the second line through the first knot.

2 Then begin to tie another figure-of-eight knot.

3 Complete the second figure-of-eight knot, which, when the work is turned end-for-end, must be identical to the first one.

4 Pull first on the working ends to remove the slack from the individual knots, then on both standing parts to slide them together.

Double Harness Bend with Parallel Ends

Many knot tyers prefer
symmetrical bends, which are
often better looking and can be
easier to learn, tie and memorize.
This version is also a little
stronger and more secure than
some asymetrical knots.

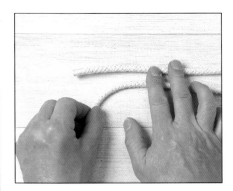

1 Place the two lines to be joined
parallel and together.

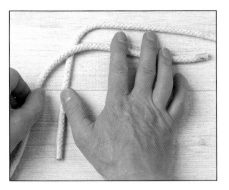

2 Take one working end down
beneath the other standing part.

3 Then bring this end up and back
over the other line.

4 Tuck the end down between
both lines to complete one half
of the knot.

5 Turn the half-completed knot end-
for-end and tie an identical crossing
knot with the other working end. Work
the knot tight, so that both ends protrude
together from the same side of the knot.

Strop Bend

Any two eyes, loops and endless strops or slings may be interlaced this way. It can amuse young children to make long multi-coloured chains of elastic bands with a series of these knots; but the strop bend can also be put to hard labour on construction sites and dockyards.

1 Bring together two bights and insert one up through the other.

2 Double the working bight of the two back upon itself.

3 Pick up the standing parts of the working loop to draw them through the secondary loop.

4 Pull the remainder of the working loop completely through itself.

5 Begin to pull the two bights in opposite directions, one away from the other.

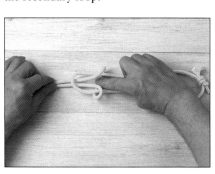

6 Continue until the two bights are snugly interlocked with one another.

7 Tighten by pulling on both pairs of loop legs at once. While this knot resembles a reef (square) knot in layout, the dynamics are very different, and it will, of course, only come undone if one of the lines breaks.

Carrick Bend with Ends Opposed

This knot name dates from the 18th century, but its actual origin is obscure. At Carrick-on-Suir in Ireland, the Elizabethan plasterwork of Ormonde Castle is embellished with numerous carrick bends moulded in relief, while a "carrack" was a type of medieval trading ship, from which perhaps comes Carrick Road outside Falmouth Harbour in Cornwall. Recommended for large hawsers and cables, this bend has acquired a reputation for strength, when it actually reduces the breaking strength of the ropes to about 65 per cent. Nevertheless, given today's strong synthetic cordages, it is still a considerable heavyweight among bends. It is said to be more secure if it is tied in such a way that the working ends emerge on opposite sides of the knot.

1 Make a loop with the working end of one of the two lines to be joined lying (in this instance) over its own standing part.

2 Place the second line over the initial loop, in the direction shown, and pass the working end beneath the other standing part.

3 Begin a second loop, taking the second working end over the first working end.

4 With the second end, make a locking tuck that goes under-over-under to complete the knot. Pull on the two standing parts to tighten the knot, when the flat heraldic outline will capsize into a compact and different form.

Heaving Line Bend

This quick and simple knot attaches a lightweight throwing line (or "messenger") to the bight or eye of a heavier hawser that is to be hauled into position. It was first mentioned in a seamanship manual of 1912.

1 Make a bight in the hawser that has to be hauled.

2 Take the lighter line and lay it over the bight.

3 Divert the working end to one side (the left in this instance), taking it around and beneath the standing part of the bight and then bringing it over its own standing part.

4 Take the working end beneath the short leg of the bight.

5 Bring the working end back to the lefthand side of the knot, tucking it finally beneath itself as shown. Note that the finished shot shows the reverse side of the completed knot.

Bowline Bend

In wet natural fibre ropes at sea, when even simple knots could be relied upon to hold, it was recommended that hawsers should be joined with a pair of interlocked bowlines, and that still holds good – literally – in some of today's cordage. The advantage of the bowline is that it does not slip or jam even under tension. This bend can be used for lines of dissimilar diameters, constructions and materials, but the two loops may be weakened where their interlinked elbows cross and rub against one another.

1 Make the initial overhand loop that will cinch the completed knot and tuck the working end up through it.

3 Tuck the working end down through the loop and pull the working end to tighten the knot.

2 Pass the working end around behind the standing part of the line.

4 Make an overhand loop with a second line and tuck the working end through the first bowline.

5 Pass the working end up through the second loop and under the standing part of the line.

6 Tuck this working end down through the second loop and pull the working end to tighten the knot.

Twin Bowline Bend

This alternative to the bowline bend avoids the sharp elbows of the latter knot and is stronger for that reason as it avoids the risk of chafing and rubbing.

1 Arrange the two lines parallel, with the working ends opposed.

2 Form the loop that is characteristic of bowlines in the standing part of one of the lines, as shown.

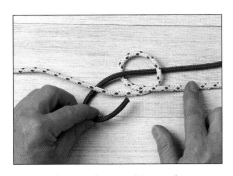

3 Tuck the other working end up through the loop and pass it around the back of the standing part.

4 Tuck the end down through the loop to complete the first bowline.

5 Turn the half-completed knot end-for-end and begin again with an identical loop.

6 Take the end and tuck it as before, up through the loop and around the standing part.

7 Tuck the end down through the loop to complete the second bowline, ensuring that the working ends are at least as long as those illustrated (and preferably longer). The standing parts will each take an equal part of the strain upon the loaded knot.

HITCHES

A line is said to be "made fast" (not "hitched") to various objects, even another rope, and only the knot itself is called a hitch. Some hitches work best with a direct pull at right angles to the point of attachment, such as the pedigree cow hitch; others will withstand a sideways or varying direction of pull. The gaff topsail halyard bend is actually a hitch and so is included within this section. Its irregular name is due to old-time sailormen who, obeying a verbal quirk, always spoke of "bending" a line to a ring or spar.

Pedigree Cow Hitch

This is a useful knot for a pull that is more or less at right angles to the point of attachment. Put it to work to start lashings or to suspend garden shed and garage impedimenta from the roof.

1 Take the working end around and down, from front to back of the anchorage point.

2 Bring the end around in front of its own standing part.

3 Take the end back up behind the foundation and bring it down in front once again.

4 Tuck the end through the bight, the result being a fairly useless common cow hitch.

5 Now tuck the working end back through the basic knot to secure and transform it.

Cow Hitch Variant

This is an even stronger and more secure version than the pedigree cow hitch. Although similar to the pedigree cow hitch, which was an innovation from the fresh mind of Harry Asher, the cow hitch variant was published in 1995 by Robert Pont of France, who first spotted it in Quebec and named it the Piwich knot after the child (Piwich Kust of the Bois Brule tribe) who tied it. Use it as a bag knot, or to suspend lockets, amulets and similar items of jewellery from a neck lanyard.

1 Take the working end once around the point of attachment.

2 Make a single half hitch with the working end around the line's standing part.

3 Take the working end across the front and pass it up (in this instance, to the left) behind the anchorage point.

4 Bring the working end down in front and tuck it down beside the standing part of the line, taking it through the enclosing turn.

Figure-of-Eight Hitch

A trivial holdfast for the odd undemanding job, this hitch is releatively simple and easy to master. The extra crossing point gives a bit more friction and hold than a single half hitch. It is more secure than a single half hitch, especially around an object with a small diameter, and could, of course, be used with a round turn, but always treat it with caution as it does not have the strength of many other hitches.

1 Pass the working end of the line around the anchorage point from front to back.

2 Bring the end forward and across the standing part (in this instance, from right to left).

3 Take the end (in this instance, from left to right) around the back of the standing part.

4 Tuck the end up through the loop to create the characteristic figure-of-eight layout.

Buntline Hitch

In effect, this is two half hitches with the second one inside the first, the working end being trapped against whatever it is tied around. This knot is for situations where the line flaps about with a tendency to shake less secure knots loose (for example, running rigging and flag halyards). A buntline was used to brail up square-sails, which flogged unmercifully, and so a very secure knot was needed. Tied in flat material, it turns out to be the common four-in-hand necktie knot that around 1860 superseded bowties for men.

1 Pass the working end through or around the anchorage point from front to back.

2 Take the end across the front and bring it around the back in a figure of eight layout.

3 Pass the end completely across the loop that has been formed.

4 Continue to take the end around to the back of the arrangement.

5 Tuck the working end through from back to front, as shown, thus forming two half hitches.

Clove Hitch, Tied in a Bight

The ease with which this knot can be tied makes it a popular one, but it comes adrift if pulled and jerked about. Then again, it can also jam, so consider adding a drawloop. Use it to suspend objects by means of lanyards or to secure a light boat to a bollard. Ashore, this knot was once known as a builder's knot.

1 Make an overhand loop at any convenient point in the line.

2 Add an underhand loop further along the line, so that the pair consists of two opposing halves.

3 Arrange the two loops so that they are the same size and close together.

4 Rotate the two loops a little in opposite directions, in order to overlap them.

5 Insert the rail, spar, rope or other foundation through both loops and pull either or both ends to tighten the resulting hitch.

KNOTS

The word "knot" has a specific meaning, apart from its general use for any cordage entanglement. Strictly speaking, it refers only to those that are not bends or hitches, namely stopper knots, shortenings, loops and bindings, as well as anything tied in string or other small stuff, such as cotton or thread. Stopper cordage knots may be used to prevent fraying but their function is primarily to prevent the cord pulling out of a pulley-block, fairlead or other opening. Shortenings are temporary devices, intended to avoid cutting rope that must later be reused. Loops may be single or multiple, fixed or sliding. Bindings can be makeshift quick seizings or semi-permanent lashings, while slide-and-grip knots are remarkable shock-absorbing contrivances.

Ashley's Stopper Knot

The overhand knot, and figure-of-eight knot, despite their increasing bulks, will all pull through a hole of about the same diameter. For a fatter stopper, use this knot devised by Clifford Ashley sometime around 1910 after he had spied a lumpy knot, which he did not recognize, aboard a boat in the local oyster fishing fleet. This was the outcome, hence his name for it (the oysterman's stopper knot). Later, when he was able to see the mystery knot close up, it proved to be nothing but a wet and badly swollen figure-of-eight knot; but Ashley's new stopper knot has survived to become a minor classic.

1 Immobilizing the end, throw an overhand loop in the standing part of the line.

2 Take the standing part of the line beneath the loop.

3 Pull a bight through the loop to create an overhand knot with a drawloop.

4 Bring the working end up and through from the back of the bight (no other way will do). Pull the standing part down until the bight traps the end tightly against the knot.

Figure-of-Eight Knot

Favoured by dinghy sailors for the ends of jib leads and main sheets, this quick and simple knot has a bit more bulk than an overhand knot and is more easily untied – but it will escape through holes of roughly the same size. In its untightened form, this familiar knot has long been associated with faithful love – an emblem of interwoven affection.

1 Make a small bight at the end of the line and impart half a twist to turn it into a loop.

2 Impart an extra half twist to bring about the figure-of-eight shape that gives this knot its name.

3 Begin to pull the working end through the loop from the top. If you wish to leave a drawloop, stop at this stage.

4 Draw the working end right the way through to complete a common figure-of-eight knot. To tighten this knot, tug first on both ends to remove slack from the knot; then pull on just the standing part, pulling the end over and trapping it against the top of the knot.

Munter Friction Hitch

An effective means of abseiling (rappelling), belaying or absorbing the energy of a fall, this friction hitch for kernmantel rope also reverses to yield slack or apply tension when needed. The rope is pressed around and through the karibiner and will break the fall of a climber by locking up, in much the same way that a car seat belt locks. Although it can be used for abseiling (rappelling), this is not generally recommended as the practice can be hard on the rope, eventually causing it to "burn". The munter friction hitch was introduced in 1974, and is also known as the Italian hitch and sliding ring hitch.

1 Use the climbing rope with an appropriate size and quality of karabiner.

2 Make a loop (exactly as illustrated) in the climbing rope.

3 Unscrew (if necessary) and open the gate of the karabiner.

4 Hook upwards with the karabiner to incorporate the climbing rope.

5 Then pass the karabiner through the initial loop from back to front (no other way will work).

6 When completed, this hitch is revealed as a dynamic crossing knot. The finished shot shows this knot from the rear side.

Double Munter Friction Hitch

Canadian rock and building climber Robert Chisnall devised and publicized this variation of the munter friction hitch. The additional turn around the karabiner creates greater friction and consequently more control over the load line. This is ideal for smaller diameter rope, which often needs more friction.

1 Choose an appropriate size and quality of karabiner to use with the climbing rope.

2 Make a double loop in the climbing rope, exactly as illustrated.

3 Hook upwards with the karabiner to incorporate the climbing rope.

4 Then pass the karabiner through the initial double loop from back to front as shown (no other way will work).

5 When completed, this hitch exerts more friction, and so will support greater loads than the basic knot.

Munter Mule

A rescuer's "extra hand", this contrivance may be a newcomer to the climbing scene. Ensure you try it out in training situations before resorting to it in trickier circumstances. Used for tying off an injured climber temporarily, this holdfast has the advantage that it can be untied while loaded. It is, in effect, a munter friction hitch – that dynamic relation of the inactive crossing knot – which has been immobilized by the addition of a slip knot backed up by an overhand knot (both tied in the bight). The munter mule's bulkiness makes it easy to undo.

1 Begin with a munter friction hitch tied on to a karabiner, and make a bight with the working end of the rope.

2 Pass the bight just made behind the standing part of the rope.

3 Bring the bight around to the front of the rope and tuck it down through its own loop.

4 Tighten the resulting overhand knot around the standing part of the rope. This is the munter mule.

5 Now take the working bight across the front of the rope, and return the bight around the back of the rope.

6 Finally tuck the working bight through its latest loop to reinforce it with a two-strand overhand knot around the standing part of the rope.

Sheepshank

The sheepshank temporarily shortens a length of rope. It will bridge an obviously damaged or a suspect section of rope, taking the strain upon the other two standing parts.

1 Fold the rope and fold it again, shortening it as required, into a flattened "S" or "Z" shape with two bights.

2 Make an incomplete overhand knot – known as a marlinespike hitch – in one standing part.

3 Pull the adjacent bight through the marlinespike hitch in a locking tuck that goes over-under-over the rope.

4 Turn the half-finished knot end-for-end and make another marlinespike hitch in the other standing part.

5 Insert the remaining bight over-under-over, securing the nearby hitch, and gently tighten both ends of the knot until they are snug and firm. Ensure that the load falls equally on all three standing parts (unless one is damaged, in which case it must lie between the other two and be slightly slacker than them).

Square Knot

Dressing gown (bath robe) cords or other waist-ties may be fastened with this knot, allowing the ends to hang down stylishly. It is best, however, in a knotted scarf, when the four-panelled knot neatly fills the V-shaped space in an open blouse or shirt. Because there is already a square knot in the United States (which the British call the reef knot), Americans refer to this knot by several other names, including the rustler's knot, the Japanese crown knot, the Japanese success knot, the Chinese cross knot, and the Chinese good luck knot.

1 Make a bight in one of two cords, or one end of a single cord, and pass it around the other cord or end.

2 Lead the second cord up behind the initial bight in the other cord.

3 Bring the second cord down in front of the first one.

4 Pass the first working end over the front of the second to make a locking tuck through the open bight. Flatten and tighten this knot by pulling a bit at a time on each of the four strands that emerge from the knot.

Crossing Knot

It could be argued that this is actually one of the simplest and most insecure of hitches, although it is rarely, if ever, classified that way in knot manuals. In fact it is inconsistencies like these that make knot lore such a fascinating field of study for devotees. Use this to brace parcel ties or to suspend a barrier rope from stake to stake at a school fete; even plastic tape at a scene of crime might be hitched from tree to lamp post to railing by means of this knot. (It is also the basis for some other, more complex knots.)

1 Cross one line over the other line or the post so that they are at right angles to one another.

2 Bring the working end back down behind the other line.

3 Take the working end across the front (from left to right in this example) of its own standing part.

4 Tuck the end up and under the other line. Tension must be maintained, since there is no locking tuck to retain the form of this arrangement.

Good Luck Knot

For a robust knot, easy to tie and tighten, this has a striking finished appearance. Use it for gift-wrapped parcels or simply hang it from a belt as a novel chatelaine for keys (keychain). The appearance of this knot will be enhanced if, between the three large loops, the four small ones are left open.

1 Middle a single length of cord and make a narrow bight in it.

2 Pull out and retain a second bight in the lefthand leg of the cord.

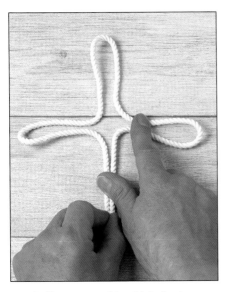

3 Pull out a matching bight in the righthand leg of the cord.

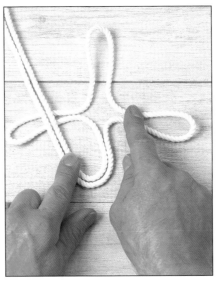

4 Lay both standing parts of the cord up and over the lefthand bight.

5 Take the lefthand bight and lay it over the upper bight.

6 Take the upper bight and lay it down over the righthand bight.

7 Tuck the righthand bight over and through beneath the two standing parts of the cord.

8 Without distorting it in any way, carefully tighten the resulting four-part crown knot.

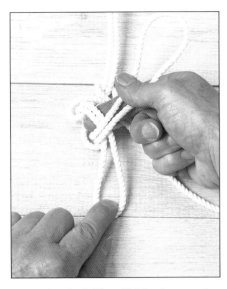

9 Bring the lefthand bight down and cross the lower bight up over it.

10 Lay the righthand bight up and over the lower bight.

11 Lead the two standing parts of the cord down in a final locking tuck through the vacant bight. Tighten the second crown knot atop the first one.

Wrapped & Reef Knotted Coil

Rope coiled this way and secured with reef (square) knots has a good chance of surviving any journey tangle-free. This is a quick and simple arrangement that serves to prevent all sorts of frustrating entanglements. It works for thick rope and smaller cordage, and is easy to untie when the rope is required.

1 Bring the two ends of the coiled rope close together, and tie a half-knot (with longer ends than are illustrated).

2 Then add a second half-knot (of opposite handedness) to complete a reef (square) knot.

3 Wrap both ends away from the reef (square) knot, with identical helixes, so as to secure the coil.

4 Where the two ends meet opposite the original reef (square) knot, tie another half-knot.

5 Then add a second half-knot (of opposite handedness) to complete a second reef (square) knot.

Alpine Coil

This is the method of securing a coil of rope for transport that is traditionally preferred by climbers and cavers.

1 Bring the two ends of the coiled rope close together.

2 Bend one end back to create a bight about 15–20 cm/6–8 in long.

3 Wrap the other end around the coiled rope, including the bight.

4 Ensure that the second wrapping turn traps and holds the initial turn.

5 Wrap fairly tightly and keep each succeeding turn snug.

6 Complete at least six wrapping turns, then tuck the working end through the bight (pulling upon the other end to secure it).

Figure-of-Eight Coil

This is the storekeeper's way of hanging coils up out of harm's way. Coiling the rope double is the trick that makes this coil fast and effective, with a practical loop to hang it by. Ropes travelling in the back of a car can always be coiled this way as they can be held in place by securing the loop around a fixed object. It is, like many of the coils, quick and easy to untie, if required in an emergency.

1 Middle the rope prior to coiling and then coil it doubled.

2 Bring the bight back upon itself so as to create a loop.

3 Lead the working bight around the back of the coil to the other side.

4 Finally tuck it up through its own loop (and the entire coil), from front to back, to make a loop from which to hang it.

Fireman's Coil

This method of forming a coil with a useful hanging loop is probably the most basic coil and deserves to be better known.

1 Bring the two ends of the coiled rope close together.

2 With one of the ends, make an overhand small loop.

3 Pass the working end through the coil and behind it, and make a bight.

4 Tuck the bight up through the loop, from behind, and gently pull it tight. Suspend the coil from this loop.

BINDINGS & LOOPS

There are two kinds of binding knot. The first is around an object with a wide diameter, where a cord, strap or fabric is wound one or more times and the two ends are then securely tied together (for example, packing parcels, securing a cloth covering to a homemade jar of preserves or applying a first aid tourniquet). The second is for narrow diameters, when a special constricting knot is applied to grip and hold with its own internal friction (for example, to prevent the cut end of a rope from fraying or to attach a hose to a tap).

A loop knot may be used like a hitch, but placed over a post or rail (rather than tied around it), the advantage being that it is easily removed again for re-use. Running knots or nooses, useful for parcels, may have originated as snares to catch animals and birds for food. Some loops are tied in the bight, others in the end of cordage.

Granny Knot

This is the commonest of knots. Everyone knows how to tie it, but there is little good to be said for it. It either slips or jams and so is totally unreliable; tied as the double granny bow with twin drawloops, it causes shoe-laces to come undone. It is included here solely to highlight its shortcomings, and thus to compare and contrast it with the reef (square), thief and grief knots.

1 Present two ends of the same cord to one another – in this instance, left over right.

2 Tie a half-knot, noting how the two entwined parts spiral to the left, that is, anticlockwise (counterclockwise).

3 Bring the two working ends together, once again left over right.

4 Tie a second half-knot in which the two entwined parts spiral clockwise (or lefthanded).

Reef Knot (Square Knot)

This flat and symmetrical knot of two interlocked bights was known to the ancient Egyptians, Greeks and Romans. With twin drawloops, it becomes the double reef (square) bow, a more secure way to tie shoe-laces. It is strictly a binding knot, reliable only when pressed against something else and tied in both ends of the same material, so restrict its use to bandages and all sorts of parcels (including reefing the sails of small craft).

NOTE – Never use it as a bend.

1 Bring two ends of the same cord together, in this case left over right.

2 Tie a half-knot and see how the two entwined knot parts spiral to the left, anticlockwise (counterclockwise).

3 Bring the two ends back together, but this time right over left.

4 Tie a second half-knot. Note that the two entwined parts helix to the right, anticlockwise (counterclockwise), the opposite of the first half-knot.

Thief Knot

At first glance this looks just like a reef (square) knot – but there is a drastic difference. The short ends are on opposite sides which, of course, cause it to slip and slide due to the uneven pull that this exerts. This renders the knot practically useless in its present form, except as a stepping stone on the way to the robust tumbling thief knot, but it makes a useful teaching aid to quiz those who think they know their knots and their applications.

1 Make a small bight in one end of the cord or line.

2 Introduce the other end through the bight just made, angling it towards the short end of the bight.

3 Lead the working end around the back of both parts of the bight.

4 Finally, tuck the working end back through the bight to emerge alongside its own standing part.

Grief Knot

Combining the characteristic failings of both granny and thief knots, this is the most insecure of knots, diagonally unbalanced and with an uneven pull from short ends on opposite sides. But there is a trick to it. Pull both ends and gently roll the knot to tighten it; then lever them on to opposite sides so that they lock solid. In this way the knot can be used to bind together garden trelliswork and similar lightweight structures.

1 Make a small bight in one end of the cord or line.

2 Tuck the working end up through the bight, angling it towards the other short end.

3 Now tuck the working end under the first part of the bight but then over the standing part of the bight.

4 Finally, return the working end back through the bight to emerge from the completed knot alongside its own standing part.

Sack/Miller's Knot

This was used in the days when grain and other granular or powdered materials were bagged up in sacks. It cannot be tied in the bight but a drawloop may be left to prevent possible damage to the bag if the knot is cut.

1 Drape a short length of cord around the neck of the bag or sack with the short end hanging down in front of the bag.

2 Move the short end at the front over to the left.

3 Wrap the longer working end up and over the neck of the bag or sack, from front to back, taking care to trap the short end in place.

4 Take the working end down around the back of the bag and bring it up at the front again.

5 Tuck the end down through the space retained between the first and second wrapping turns and pull it snug and tight. Leave a drawloop, if preferred.

Constrictor Knot, Tied with an End

The constrictor knot can be the best of binding knots. Use it with or without a drawloop as a semi-permanent seizing on rope's ends, hose-pipes, and for every odd job imaginable. The ancient Greeks may have used it for surgical slings, and it could well be the "gunner's knot" that in later centuries seized the necks of flannel-bag gunpowder cartridges for muzzle-loading artillery. It was re-discovered and popularized by Clifford Ashley in 1944. Use this tying method when the end of the foundation rope, spar or whatever, is not easily accessible. If you wish to remove a constrictor – without nicking or scarring whatever lies beneath it – you must carefully sever the overriding diagonal with a sharp knife, and then the knot will drop neatly off in two curly cut segments.

1 Take a short length of cord or twine (hard-laid to bind softer objects, such as rope; soft and stretchy for unyielding foundations) and arrange it around whatever is to be tied.

2 Bring the working end of the binding cord up and across to the right over its own standing part.

3 Lead the end down at the back and up once more at the front.

4 Tuck the working end beneath the diagonal made earlier, completing a clove hitch.

5 Locate and loosen the upper lefthand knot part, preparatory to tucking in the working end.

6 Bring the working end across and tuck it from left to right through the loosened bight. Pull both ends in opposite directions to tighten this knot as hard as possible, when the ends may be cut off quite close to the knot.

Constrictor Knot, Tied in the Bight

This is another example of the excellent constrictor knot. Tie it more quickly this way when the end of the foundation rope, spar, or whatever, is accessible. When pulled tight it will lock securely. With practice, a constrictor knot tied by this method can be applied quicker than the eye can follow the actions.

1 Lead the working end of a short length of cord or twine, from front to back, over the object to be seized.

2 Lift the working end so as to complete a full turn.

3 Pull a fairly long bight down from the lower part of the turn just made.

4 Lift the bight and half-twist it (as shown) to place it over the end of the foundation.

5 Heave on both ends, as strongly as the cord or twine will withstand, to tighten the knot; then cut off the ends close to the knot.

Transom Knot

Clifford Ashley originally made this knot to seize together two cross-sticks for his daughter's kite. It is an adaptation of the constrictor knot and can be used for any light trelliswork. If greater strength is needed, add a second knot facing the first one and at right angles to it.

1 The components to be lashed with this knot need to be at right angles.

2 Lead the working end over the horizontal uppermost element of the construction and around the back of the vertical piece.

3 Bring the end diagonally down and across over its own standing part.

4 Now lead it around the back of the vertical piece beneath the horizonal section and return it to the front of the work once more.

5 Tuck the end through beneath the diagonal knot part, so as to form a half-knot with the two opposing cord ends. Pull as tight as possible.

Double Constrictor Knot

This variation of the constrictor knot has extra internal friction and grip; it is also more suitable for binding objects with a larger diameter, or when the objects are an awkward shape and will not automatically pull together. When tying a particularly awkward package and hands are not enough to tighten this seizing as much as required, attach each end of the cord to a screwdriver or similar handle by means of a pile hitch to apply extra leverage.

1 Wrap the cord around the item to be secured. Bring the working end diagonally up and take it across over its own standing part.

2 Lead the working end down behind the work and then up in front once more, taking care to keep between the standing part and the initial turn.

3 Take the working end up and around the foundation again, doubling the characteristic diagonal that overlays the single version of this knot.

4 Put the working end directly down behind, to emerge at the front (on the righthand side of its standing part).

5 Tuck the end through the two turns so it is parallel and to the right of its own standing part.

6 Locate and loosen the upper lefthand part of this almost completed knot, preparatory to the final tuck.

7 Bring the working end across and tuck it from left to right through the loosened bight.

8 Pull the knot as tight as possible and cut the ends off close to the knot.

Figure-of-Eight Loop

Referred to by sailormen once upon a time as a Flemish loop, the figure-of-eight loop was viewed by them with disfavour because it tended to jam in wet hemp or manilla ropes and could not easily be untied after loading. Cavers and climbers now prefer this versatile alternative to the bowline. It is easily tied – even by an uncertain beginner – and readily checked by a team leader (in the poorest light and the worst weather). Tie the working end to the standing part for added security.

1 Make a generous bight in the end of the cord or rope.

2 Impart half a twist in the bight to create twin loops, as shown.

3 Add an extra half-twist to the loops already produced, as shown.

4 Tuck the bight through the twin loops and work the completed knot neatly snug and tight.

Manharness Knot

This is an ancient knot, although as recently as 1992 American Mike Storch recommended a series of these knots spaced out along a picket line to tether horses. It is tied in the bight.

1 Make an anticlockwise (counterclockwise) overhand loop.

2 Bring the upper section of line around to the back of the loop.

3 Press the righthand side of the original loop to the left beneath the middle (rearward) knot part.

4 Then pull it further left, over the lefthand side of the loop.

5 Hold onto the loop and pull the knot to tighten it.

Alpine Butterfly

This is a European mountaineering classic middleman's tie-on. If, as A.P. Herbert (1890–1971) wrote in a poem, "the bowline is the king of knots", then the Alpine butterfly, added Scouting's ropework writer John Sweet, must surely be the queen. Its other name, given to it by Clifford Ashley, is the lineman's loop. It is tied in the bight.

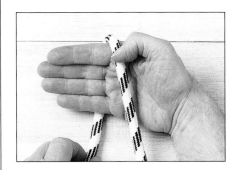

1 Lay a bight of rope over one hand at the point where the knot is required.

2 Lead the working part of the rope around the hand a second time to complete one round turn.

3 Add a third turn with the rope around the hand.

4 Pick up (from the top of the hand) the middle one of the three turns.

5 Carry this over to become the lefthand rope part.

6 Tuck the lefthand rope part through (from left to right) beneath the other two turns.

7 Pull out a bight of the required size and then pull on both standing parts of the rope to tighten the knot.

Bowstring Knot

Limited adjustment makes this knot suitable for small roles such as tightening or slackening tent guy lines or washing lines. It has been used to improvise the sliding loop on American cowboys' lassoes and the lariats of the Spanish vaqueros; while the ancient Briton, Lindow Man – whose 2,000-year-old mummified remains are now displayed in the British Museum, London – was strangled with a similar knot.

1 With the working end of a rope, make a clockwise underhand loop.

2 Tuck the working end through the loop to produce an overhand knot.

3 Take the working end through the end compartment of the overhand knot, ensuring that the over-under sequence is precisely as shown (no other way will do).

4 Tighten the knot, adding a small stopper knot to prevent the end from pulling free.

Midshipman's Hitch

This is a slide-and-grip knot, which may be grasped and slid by hand to where it is required (after which it holds firm), making it suitable for tensioning guy lines, stays or shrouds. The name implies a Royal Navy origin.

1 Make a clockwise overhand loop of approximately the required size.

2 Bring the working end around and tuck it from the back through the loop just formed.

3 Take the working end up and begin a wrapping turn, which must cross and trap its own earlier turn.

4 Bring the working end once again through the loop and continue to wrap it (towards the standing part).

5 Take the working end up and around the standing part, so that two turns now diagonally overlay and trap the original turn.

6 Lead the working end outside the loop and take it from left to right across the front of the standing part.

7 Finally, create a half hitch around the standing part of the line and tighten it so that it lies alongside the other riding turns.

Arbor Knot

Primarily a knot attaching monofilament or braid to an arbor (a reel or spool), this knot is also used as a shock-absorbing slide-and-grip knot when securing a line to a hook or lure.

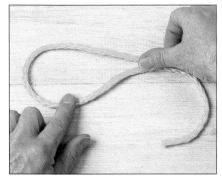

1 Make a bight near to one end of the monofilament, braid or other line.

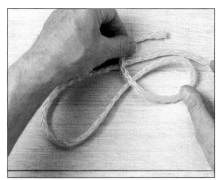

2 Keeping the two parallel line parts close together, form a small loop by laying the working end across them.

3 Continue by taking the working end down behind the emerging knot.

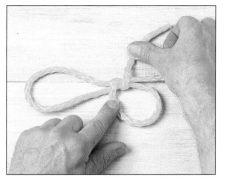

4 Bring the end up out of the loop and complete a round turn of the two bight parts.

5 Take the working end down behind the knot once more.

6 Complete a second turn, keeping the wrappings tight as they are tied.

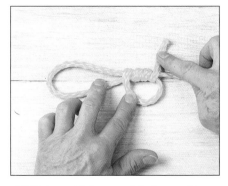

7 Take a third turn with the working end, ensuring that all are snug against one another. Tighten the small loop, and trap the end by pulling on one of the large loop legs.

Adjustable Loop

Another creation from Canadian climber Robert Chisnall, this loop can easily be shifted by hand in either direction – but it seizes when loaded. A safety feature of this knot (and of all slide-and-grip knots) is that shock loading will cause it to slide until friction reduces the load to a manageable percentage, when it will hold.

1 Make a loop with the working end laid over the standing part.

2 With the working end, take a turn around the standing part.

3 Take a second turn around the standing part with the working end.

4 Now pass the working end around both legs of the loop.

5 Finally, tuck the working end beneath the second wrapping turn.

Portuguese Bowline

Old-time sailormen were a polyglot tribe who shipped aboard any vessel that would have them, so knot names spread haphazardly. Felix Reisenberg called this a French bowline; whereas Clifford Ashley, who spotted it aboard Portuguese boats in his home town of New Bedford, Massachusetts, gave it the current name. It was used as a kind of boatswain's chair, with the crewman's legs through one loop and his back supported by the other one.

1 Form a small overhand loop with the working end of the rope.

2 Make a large loop in the same direction and of roughly the required working size.

3 As the working end approaches the smaller loop, take it behind.

4 Bring it up and through the cinch as if tying a common bowline.

5 Take the end around the back of the standing part of the rope.

6 Finally, tuck the end down through the cinch and tighten the resulting knot around the two trapped loop parts. Ensure the end is longer than illustrated.

Portuguese Bowline with Splayed Loops

A couple of these versatile knots will sling a plank or ladder as an improvised work platform, but note that each one of the two loops can pull slack from the other. Do not use this knot in circumstances where this may prove an undesirable feature. An illustration of this knot appeared in *Tratado de Apparelho do Navio*, (1896), Lisbon, and Clifford Ashley reports having first seen it used aboard Portuguese ships.

1 Arrange the line as shown in the illustration above.

2 Reduce the size of the lower loop, secure the lefthand bight, and bring the working end around to create a second loop on the righthand side of the emerging knot.

3 Tuck the working end up through the small central loop and then take the end around behind the standing part of the rope.

4 Finally, tuck the end down through the central loop or cinch. Adjust the two working loops to the required size, and then begin to tighten the familiar bowline layout.

Tom Fool's Knot

This is one of many so-called handcuff knots that, according to knot lore, can render any Houdini helpless. In fact, they were probably used for hobbling farm animals overnight, as an alternative to a picket line, so as to leave them free to graze. Tie this knot in the bight.

1 Cast a clockwise overhand loop, tying it in the bight of the chosen rope or cord.

2 Add an anticlockwise (counterclockwise) underhand loop, of similar size to the first one.

3 Partly overlap the two loops, the lefthand one in front of the righthand one, and prepare to pull the leading edge of the lefthand loop (from the front to the back) through the righthand loop, at the same time pulling the leading edge of the righthand loop (from the back to the front) through the lefthand loop.

4 Pull out twin loops, adjust them to the required size, then tighten the knot.

Handcuff Knot

This takes a second or so more to tie than the simple Tom Fool's knot since the twin loops are interlocked, but it is doubtful that this more elaborate version is stronger or more stable than the simpler knot.

1 Cast a clockwise overhand loop, tying it in the bight of the rope.

2 Add a second loop, anticlockwise (counterclockwise) and underhand.

3 Partly overlap the loops, with the righthand one coming in front of the lefthand one.

4 Pull the leading edge of the lefthand loop (from the back to the front) through the righthand loop; at the same time pull the leading edge of the righthand loop (from the front to the back) through the lefthand loop.

5 Adjust the loops to the required size and then tighten the knot.

MATS, PLAITS, RINGS, SLINGS & THINGS

Knots are like tools. It is possible to muddle along with four or five, using and misusing them for every task imaginable. The best strategy, however, is to acquire a full and varied repertoire of bends, hitches and other contrivances, so that you always have precisely the correct combination for the job in hand. There are many knots, bends and hitches that may be used only infrequently; but, when they are, nothing else will do as well. What follows is a selection of these occasional knots.

Barrel Sling

Use this split form of the overhand knot to hoist or lower an open barrel, cask or drum that is partly full. The working end must be secured to the standing part of the rope, and care must also be taken to ensure that the bottom loop is unable to slip from beneath the load. This sling appears barely adequate for the job, yet it was once a handy favourite with crews shifting cargoes of tubs, casks and barrels.

1 Place the lifting line beneath the load and tie a half knot on top.

2 Split the half knot in two and work each knot part down over the load.

3 Pull both legs of the divided knot snug around the load.

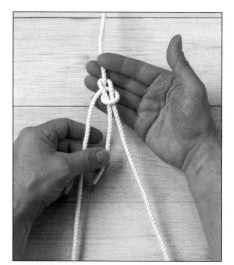

4 Finally, tie a bowline in the shorter end to the standing part.

Plank Sling

A grown-up relative of pole lashings but made with ropes rather than cords. A couple of plank slings will improvise a working platform.

1 Place one end of the rope beneath the plank or other staging.

2 Push an extra bight beneath the plank, making an "S" or "Z" shape.

3 Bring one end of the rope across and tuck it through the bight on the opposite side of the plank.

4 Take the other end across and tuck it through the opposite bight.

5 Adjust and tighten the sling so that the tips of the bights are just above the edges of the plank, on the working surface; then tie the shorter end to the standing part of the rope.

Half Hitching

Long parcels of many different shapes and sizes (from carpets to lengths of plastic plumbing from a do-it-yourself store) may be tied with a series of half hitches to secure them. Once you have tied the first binding loop, continue to arrange them so that they are spaced at neat and regular intervals and the pressure on the surface of the parcel is consistent. Apply gentle tension by means of the crossing knots on the return journey.

1 Make a sliding loop around the goods, from a small fixed loop with the long end tucked through it.

2 Cast an underhand loop (clockwise, in this instance), tying it in the bight.

3 Slip the loop over the end of the parcel and pull the resulting half hitch tight.

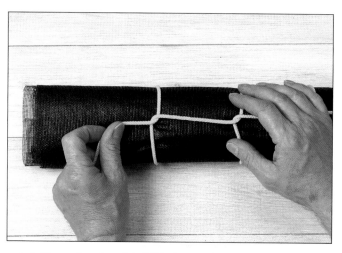

4 Add a series of such half hitches, tied in the bight, tightening them so that they are aligned and equidistant from one another.

5 Turn the work over, when the end is reached, and – at the first crossing point – tie a crossing knot.

6 Add a series of such crossing knots, tensioning each one so as to retain the spacing of the original half hitches.

7 Go around the other end of the parcel, and tie off to the original small fixed loop.

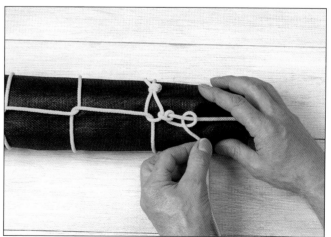

8 Finally, complete the package by tying off with a couple of half hitches.

Marline Hitching

Marline hitching looks identical to half hitching, but it is in fact very different. Try sliding both kinds off: half hitching collapses to nothing, which means that it can be tied in the bight, while marline hitching emerges as a string of overhand knots (and so requires a working end). This method tends to cling better during the tying process, but is somewhat slower to do than the simpler half hitching. Use it to lash up a garden hammock for winter storage or a carpet when moving house, and to parcel any other awkwardly long load.

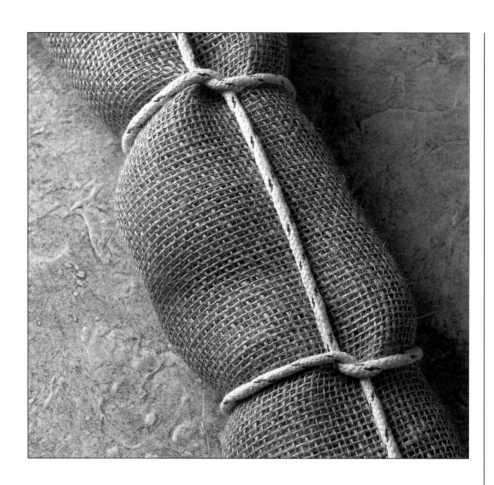

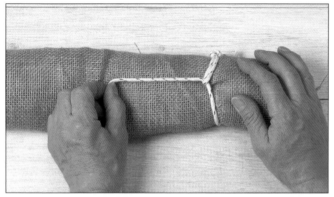

1 Start with a sliding noose around the goods, tied from a small fixed loop with the working end passed through it.

2 Tie an overhand knot around the parcel, using the working end.

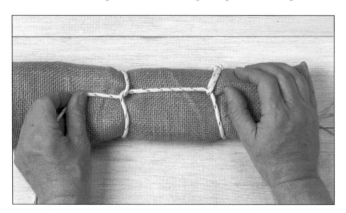

3 Pull the overhand knot tight, when, unlike mere half hitching, the extra friction will tend to hold the surrounding knot in place.

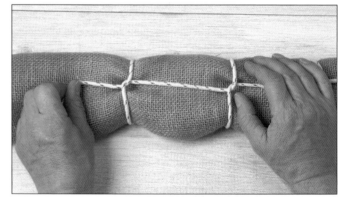

4 Add a series of such overhand knots, spaced evenly along the length of the parcel. Turn the work over and return to the starting place with a series of crossing knots and tie off.

Underhand Loop Hitching

The spine that emerges from this covering is a kind of chain stitch best fitted for a thicker ring. This – and other ring hitchings – may be executed in fairly fine twines and cords by needleworkers or by rope workers in wool, cottons or silks. They are also applied with substantial leather thongs by leather workers. It is a very versatile technique. This kind of hitching looks similar to a knitting stitch, but knitted items can unravel, whereas this pattern is composed of individual knots, each of which is separately and securely tied and, unlike knitting stitches, is not reliant on the preceding knots or stitches. Use it on light pulls or curtain cords.

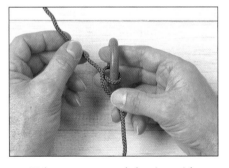

1 Take a turn around the ring with the cord and cross the two parts, the standing end up and the working end down.

2 Form a clockwise underhand loop with the working part of the cord.

3 Pass the working end through the ring (from right to left).

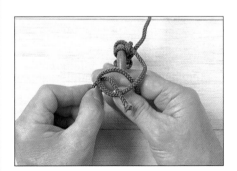

4 Tuck the end up through the underhand loop, and draw the knotting snug and tight.

5 Continue to wrap around the ring and tuck through underhand loops.

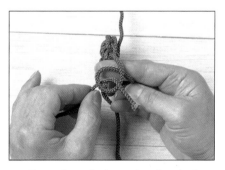

6 Reproduce the looped and tucked pattern until the ring is covered.

111

Alternate Ring Hitching

Large metal rings may be hitched over to prevent them banging and clanging against hard surfaces. Smaller ones make decorative finger-holds for blind pulls, etc. Needleworkers with stamina may make dozens or hundreds of very fine ones and then stitch them together to produce lace or tatted-like wall hangings or quilts.

1 Thread a length of cord and thread it on to the ring to be covered.

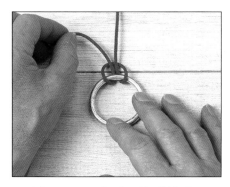

2 Tie a reversed pair of half hitches, resembling a bale sling hitch.

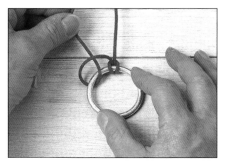

3 Add a third half hitch, which must be the mirror-image of the second one, and pulled tight up against it.

4 Add a fourth half hitch, which must be the mirror-image of the third, and therefore the same as the second.

5 Repeat steps 2 to 4 as often as required to cover the ring completely with the cord.

Continuous Ring Hitching

This results in a slim spine and works best on rings of small cross-section.

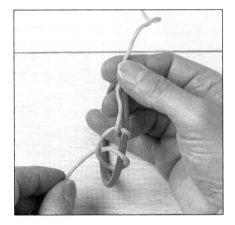

1 Tie two identical half hitches, which will resemble a clove hitch.

2 Add a third half hitch, taking care to wrap and tuck the working end in the same direction as the previous pair.

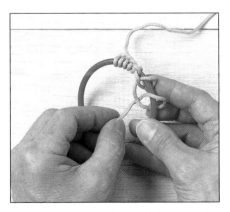

3 Straighten out the work at intervals, to ensure that the spine does not spiral around the ring; this also serves to tighten the knotting.

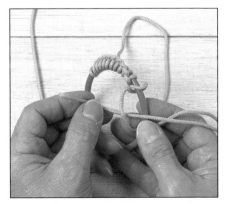

4 Continue to half hitch around the ring, always in the same direction.

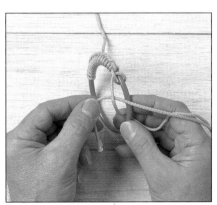

5 Keep hitching and regularly straightening the spine until the ring is completely covered. The ends can be plaited, as shown in the finished picture.

Simple Chain

This simple chain will shorten an over-long rope or cord by about one-third. It will also embellish a fine twine, to make an attractive cord to retain reading glasses, for example.

1 Cast an anticlockwise (counter-clockwise) overhand loop with a long working end.

2 Lay the working end beneath the loop and pull a bight (from back to front) through it; then pull the resulting knot tight.

3 Pull a second bight in the working end through the first bight and pull it tight.

4 Similarly, pull a third bight through the second bight and pull it tight.

5 Continue pulling, bight through bight, tightening each stage before going on to the next.

6 To finish the chain, simply tuck the working end through the preceding bight. This will secure the completed chain sufficiently.

Endless Simple Chain

This is a very neat way to join the ends of a simple chain, ensuring that it keeps the same shape even on the join. It makes an original bracelet, necklace or anklet, and it may even be used to frame a picture or mirror. The steps are illustrated in two different colours but this chain is usually made with two ends of one cord.

1 Bring the beginning and end of one or two simple chains together.

2 Tuck the final end – in this instance, the lefthand one – up through the starting loop (from the back to the front), alongside the standing end.

3 Take the working end up (from the back to the front) through its own loop, beside itself.

4 Pass the end to the right, down (from front to back) through the adjacent loop made by step 3.

5 Withdraw the standing end from the first of its tucks and replace it with the working end.

Braid Knot

It is possible, using this single-strand knot, to replicate the familiar three-strand pigtail plait (braid); which can then be employed to shorten rope or cord, or to decorate it. The braid knot also makes a practical makeshift handle for a suitcase or sailing dinghy daggerplate.

1 Cast a long clockwise underhand loop, with three parallel cord parts.

2 Begin the plait (braid) by bringing the righthand strand over the middle strand, to lie inside and below the lefthand strand.

3 Then take the lefthand strand over the middle strand, to lie inside and below the righthand strand.

4 Repeat step 2, noting how the outermost (furthest away) strand becomes the working one each time.

5 Repeat step 3, complying once more with the principle that the least used strand becomes the next working one.

6 Continue plaiting alternate right and lefthand strands, pulling each step tight as the work develops.

7 Untangle, by pulling out the single long working end, the loose mirror-image that inevitably accumulates during the plaiting (braiding) process.

8 Tighten and tension the plait (braid) so that one final loop remains at the end.

9 Finally, tuck the working end through the remaining loop to secure the plait (braid).

Three-Strand Braid

This is the most common type of braid. Lashings and lanyards can quickly be made from smaller stuff by this means; horses' tails or long human hair can also be made orderly with it.

1 Bind three strands together and separate them into a lefthand single strand and a righthand pair of strands.

2 Bring the outermost one of the right-hand pair across (over the front) to lie inside and below the lefthand strand.

3 Take the outermost one of the lefthand pair of strands and bring it across (over the front) to lie inside and below the righthand strand.

4 Repeat step 2, pulling and tightening the work as it develops.

5 Repeat step 3, pulling with an even tension as the work develops.

6 Repeat step 2, always taking (as the latest working strand) the one of the pair furthest away.

7 Continue plaiting (braiding) with alternate strands until the desired length is reached. Knot or bind the ends securely together to prevent them from coming undone.

Four-Strand Braid

This makes a flat lashing or lanyard which, in stiff stuff, will result in a detailed network of ornamental openwork.

1 Middle two lengths of rope or cord, looping one over the other (as shown), and separating the four strands into a lefthand and a righthand pair.

2 Simultaneously, cross the lefthand pair of strands (left over right) and the righthand pair (also left over right).

3 Then cross the innermost two strands (right over left).

4 Repeat steps 2 and 3, with tension and tightness to ensure a symmetrical pattern develops.

5 Continue this process until the desired length has been reached. Bind the ends together.

Four-Strand Plait

Use good quality cords to make a lead for a small dog, a lavatory or light pull, or a waist-tie for an informal garment. This is the plait (braid) that may be seen attached to the handset of vintage telephones. It may also be used to quadruple the strength of smaller cordage when no thicker cord or rope is available.

1 Bind four strands together and sub-divide them into a lefthand and a righthand pair; then take the outer one of the righthand pair across (behind), tucking it up through and between the two lefthand strands, and returning it to lie inside and below its original righthand companion.

2 Similarly, lead the outer lefthand strand around behind, to emerge between the two righthand strands, and return to lie inside and below its lefthand partner.

3 Repeat step 1, continuing to pull and tighten the paired strands as the work progresses.

4 Repeat step 2, ensuring an even tension as the work develops.

5 Continue this regular plaiting (braiding) process, with alternate outer strands, until the required length is reached. Bind the ends together.

Three-Way Sheet Bend

For a three-way bridle of converging lines, consider this simple yet effective solution. It was first reported in 1990 by the Swedish marine artist and knotting writer Frank Rosenow, who spotted it while cruising in Greek waters.

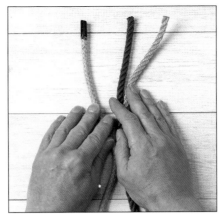

1 Bring together three pieces of rope, which may be of dissimilar size and texture.

2 Make a bight in one of the lines – the larger or stiffer, if there is one.

3 Tuck both of the other lines up through the bight.

4 Wrap the two lines around the bight and tuck them beneath themselves, so that all three working ends are on the same side of the finished knot.

Round Mat

This knotted roundel can replace an ordinary mat, or it may be glued as ornamentation or embellishment to items as diverse as a collage picture or a drum majorette's uniform.

1 Middle a length of cord and cast an anticlockwise (counterclockwise) overhand loop in the working end.

2 Bring the working end down behind the loop and arrange a symmetrical pretzel layout.

3 Pick up the other end of the cord and tuck it diagonally (up and to the left) over/under/over.

4 Lead the working end around clockwise and tuck diagonally (down and to the right) under/over/under/over.

5 Tuck the end alongside the standing part. Follow the original lead around to double or triple the knot ply. Glue or stitch the end in place on the underside.

Carrick Mat

This can be used as an actual mat, or as a component of other art and craft work. Made around the hand, the same knot can form a necktie ring.

1 Cast a clockwise overhand loop in a length of cord or rope.

2 Bring the working end down over the original loop and arrange a pretzel layout.

3 Pass the working end around (from right to left), keeping it behind the standing part.

4 Tuck it clockwise around and through the knot going over/under/over/under.

5 Tuck the working end alongside and parallel to the standing part. Follow the original lead around to double or triple the knot ply.

Glossary

ABSEIL A climber's self-controlled descent of an anchored – and often retrievable – climbing rope.

ANCHORAGE Boating – a general term that refers to moorings and the bending of cordage (by means of hitches) to various attachments; climbing – a safe belaying point.

ARAMIDES The first commercial manmade (synthetic) fibres do not melt when heated. Their high cost limits them to specialized applications.

BARREL KNOT see Blood Knot.

BELAY Boating – to make fast to a cleat or pin, often with a round turn followed by a figure-of-eight (or two) and then another round turn; climbing – the method of securing a climber in case of a fall.

BEND A name given to any one of the knots that bind (bend) two separate ropes together.

BIGHT A slack part of rope or other cordage between the two ends, particularly when it forms a partial loop.

BLOOD KNOT Any one of the strong and secure knots that depend upon numerous wrapping turns, favoured by anglers, cavers and climbers. (The name is derived from a limited surgical use.)

BRAID A term generally interchangeable with plait; but one that is sometimes stated to refer only to strands interwoven to make a flat pattern. (See also Plait.)

BREAKING STRENGTH The manufacturer's estimation of the load a rope will bear before it ruptures, expressed in kilograms and tonnes, taking no account of wear and tear, shock loading or knots that may reduce the figure drastically. (See also Safe Working Load.)

CABLE Strictly speaking, three righthanded hawsers (laid up lefthanded) make a nine-strand cable; but the term may also be loosely applied to any large length of rope.

CAPSIZE What occurs when a knot layout is distorted due to overloading, misuse or careless tightening. It may also be done deliberately as a means of quick release.

CARABINER See Karabiner.

CORD Small stuff under 10 mm/⁵⁄₁₂ in diameter.

CORE Fibres, yarns and laid or braided materials that inertly fill the unwanted space at the heart of a four (or more) strand rope, or that actively contribute desirable qualities, such as strength or elasticity to sheath-and-core ropes.

DOG To improvise a temporary running eye by making a bight in the working end of cord, around its own standing part, and then tucking the end several times to trap it in place.

EFFICIENCY The actual strength of a knot in a rope or cord, expressed as a percentage of its theoretical breaking strength.

ELBOW Two crossing points created by an extra twist in a loop.

EYE A small round loop.

FIBRE The smallest element in all vegetable rope and cordage.

FILAMENT See Monofilament.

FRAY The accidental or deliberate unlaying of a rope's end to its component strands, yarns and fibres, multi- or monofilaments.

HARD LAID Stiff cordage.

HAWSER Any three-strand rope.

HEART See Core.

HITCH Any knot used to make a line fast to an anchorage such as a rail, spar, post, ring or another rope.

KARABINER A D-shaped or pear-shaped metal snap-ring, with a pivoting gate that can be securely closed, used by cavers and climbers.

KERNMANTEL Climbing rope construction consisting of a core (or kern), often of parallel bunches of fibres contained within a tightly woven protective sheath.

KINK A damaging deformation caused by an over-tight loop.

KNOT The term for stoppers, loops and self-sufficient bindings (thus excluding bends or hitches); also the generic word for all rope and cordage tucks and ties.

LANYARD A short length of cord that is used to lash, secure or suspend an object.

LAY The direction in which rope strands spiral as they go away from from the viewer, either clockwise (righthanded, Z-laid) or anticlockwise/counterclockwise (lefthanded, S-laid).

LEAD (Pronounced "leed") The direction taken by the working end as it goes around or through an object or knot.

LINE Any rope with a specific function (for example, a tow line or washing line).

LOCKING TUCK The concluding lead of a working end that secures any knot in its finished form, without which it would unravel or collapse.

LOOP A bight with a crossing point.

MAKE FAST To attach a line to an anchorage or belay (often with a hitch).

MESSENGER The name for a throwing or heaving line when it is used to pull a thicker cord or rope across an intervening space.

MIDDLE Used as a verb, to double a rope or cord so as to locate its centre.

MONOFILAMENT Continuous synthetic fibre of uniform diameter and circular cross-section larger than 50 micons/$\frac{1}{500}$ in. (See also Multifilament.)

MULTIFILAMENT Very fine continuous synthetic fibre of uniform diameter and circular cross section less than 50 microns/$\frac{1}{500}$ in. (See also Monofilament.)

NATURAL FIBRE Processed plant products used to make rope and other cordage.

NIP The point within a knot where friction may be concentrated.

NOOSE A free-running, sliding or adjustable loop.

NYLON The first synthetic (manmade) fibre of merit available to the cordage industry. There are two grades: Nylon 66 is extensively used in the UK and USA; Nylon 6 (made available under trade names such as Perlon and Enkalon) is widely used in Europe and Japan, as well as being available in the UK and USA.

OVERHAND LOOP A loop (clockwise or anticlockwise/ counterclockwise) in which the working end is laid on top of the standing part. (See also Loop.)

PLAIT A term generally interchangeable with braid, but which can refer only to interwoven strands forming a pattern that is three-dimensional in cross-section. (See also Braid.)

POLYESTER A widely used synthetic cordage (trade names Dacron and Terylene).

POLYETHYLENE A polyolefin synthetic (manmade) fibre (commonly known as Polythene/plastic).

POLYPROPYLENE A versatile polyolefin synthetic fibre.

PRUSIKING To climb a rope using a knot that jams when downward pressure is applied but can slide up the rope when the weight is removed.

RAPPEL See Abseil.

REEF Boating – to reduce sail area in strong winds (verb); each individual fold or roll of sail taken in (noun).

ROPE Cordage over 10 mm/$\frac{5}{12}$ in in diameter.

ROUND TURN In which a working end completely encircles a ring, rail, post or rope, and finishes up alongside its own standing part. (See also Turn.)

S-LAID Lefthanded (anticlockwise/ counterclockwise).

SAFE WORKING LOAD The estimated load a rope may withstand, taking into account various weakening factors (wear and tear, damage, effect of knots and other uses); it may be as little as one-seventh the quoted breaking strength. (See Breaking Strength.)

SECURITY The integral stability of a knot.

SLING An endless rope or webbing (tape) band or strop.

SMALL STUFF A casual term for any cordage, not rope.

SOFT LAID Any flexible rope and cordage.

SPLIT FILM Synthetic (manmade), ribbon-like fibres produced from a plastic sheet.

STANDING END The inactive end of cord. (See also Working End.)

STANDING PART That part of a rope or cord anywhere between working and standing ends.

STAPLE FIBRES Graded natural fibres of limited length and strength, due to their plant origins; also discontinuous synthetic (manmade) fibres created by cutting filaments into discrete lengths.

STRAND The largest element of a rope, made from contra-twisted yarns.

STRENGTH The integral ability of knotted cordage to withstand a load.

STRING Relatively cheap and disposable small cord and twine.

STROP See Sling.

SYNTHETIC ROPE Cordage that is made from synthetic (manmade) multifilaments, monofilaments, staple fibres or split film.

TAG END Angling – working end.

THIMBLE A metal or plastic lining for an eye.

THREAD Fine line.

TURN A 360 degree wrap around a rig, rail, post or rope. (See also Round Turn.)

UNDERHAND LOOP A loop in which the working end is laid beneath the standing part.

WHIPPING A binding to prevent a rope's end from fraying.

WORKING END The active end of a rope or cord. (See also Standing End.)

YARN The basic element of rope strands, spun from natural fibres or synthetic (manmade) materials.

Z-LAID Righthanded (clockwise).

Index

Further Information

SUPPLIERS

English Braids, Spring Lane, Malvern WR14 1AL
Tel: 01684 892 222
Fax: 01684 892 111
Their marine sales division caters for the recreational sector and sail boat racing. Suppliers of barrier ropes, starter cords, shock cords, whipping twines, webbing and web-lash securing systems, and stainless steel hollow fids. Contact them for the location of your nearest stockist.

Eurorope Limited, 4 Phoenix Court, Atkinson Way, Foxhills Industrial Estate, Scunthorpe DN15 8QJ
Tel: 01724 280 480
Fax: 01724 857 750
Wholesale suppliers of rope, cord, twines, nets, lifting gear slings and accessories. Contact them for the location of your nearest stockist.

Des & Liz Pawson, Footrope Knots, 501 Wherstead Road, Ipswich, Suffolk IP2 8LL
Tel: 01473 690 090
Suppliers of traditional rope, cordage and smaller stuff; wire rope and chain; canvas; tools; fittings; fenders, knotboards, chest beckets and other knotwork; books (new, secondhand and rare). Their unique ropework museum may be visited free (by prior arrangement).

Kevin Keatley, K.J.K. Ropeworks, Town Living Farmhouse, Puddington, Tiverton, Devon EX16 8LW
Tel/fax: 01884 860 692
Supplier of cords and fittings, especially braided synthetics. Price list on request.

Leanda, 39 Borrowdale Drive, Norwich, Norfolk NR1 4LY
Tel/fax: 01603 434 707
Textile craft equipment manufacturers; specialists in Japanese-style braiding and passementerie equipment; accessories for spinning and weaving; also a book list.

Marlow Ropes Ltd, Diplocks Way, Hailsham, East Sussex BN27 3JS
Tel: 01323 847 234
Fax: 01323 440 093
email: yachting@marlow ropes.com
Website: http://www.marlow ropes.com
Market leaders in yacht rope technology and such accessories as shockcord, barrier ropes, toestrap and buoyancy bag webbing, whipping twine, splicing kits, sail repair tapes.

Ann Norman, Sagaman, Aston Road, Bampton, Oxfordshire, OX18 2AL
Tel/fax: 01993 850 823
email: sagaman@compuserve.com
Designer, handweaver and maker of cords, including four-strand cords, and ropes of traditional laid structure. Advice offered and commissions accepted.

Oakhurst Quality Products Limited, Warsop Trading Estate, Hever Road, Edenbridge, Kent TN8 5LD
Tel: 01732 866 668
Fax: 01732 864 555
Wholesale suppliers of rope, twine, cordage, chain, doormats, work gloves, garden sundries. Contact Brenda Risdon for the location of your nearest stockist.

BIBLIOGRAPHY

Asher, Harry, *The Alternative Knot Book* (Nautical Books, A. & C. Black, London, 1989)
Ashley, Clifford Warren, *The Book of Knots* (Doubleday, New York, 1944/Faber & Faber, London, 1947)
Bailey, Hazel, *Knotting for Guides* (Girl Guides Association, London, 1987)
Chisnall, Robert (Editor), *Rock Climbing Safety Manual* (Ontario Rock Climbing Association, Canada, 1984)
Day, Cyrus Lawrence, *Quipus & Witches' Knots* (University of Kansas Press, 1967)
Graumont, Raoul, and Hensel, John, *The Encyclopaedia of Knots and Fancy Rope Work* (Cornell Maritime Press, Cambridge, Maryland, 1939)
Graves, Richard H., *The Bushcraft Handbooks* (Graves, Sydney, 1952)
Griend, P. van de, and Turner, J.C. (eds), *The History and Science of Knots* (World Scientific Publishing Company, Singapore, New Jersey, London, Hong Kong, 1996)
I.G.K.T., *Knotting Matters* (1982 to the present)
Kreh, Lefty, and Sosin, Mark, *Practical Fishing & Boating Knots* (A. & C. Black, London, 1975)
Luebben, Craig, *Knots for Climbers* (Chockstone Press, Evergreen, Colorado, 1993)
March, Bill, *Mountain Rope Techniques* (Cicerone Press, Cumbria, 1983)
Noonan, Michael, *Climbing Knots – for Lefties and Righties* (I.C.S. Books, Merryville, Indiana, 1997)
Padgett, Allen, & Smith, Bruce, *On Rope* (National Speliological Society, Huntsville, Alabama, 1992)
Payne, Lee and Bob, "The Forgotten Zeppelin Knot" (*Boating Magazine*, March 1976)
Perkins, Andy, Tapes, *Slings & Harnesses* (Troll Safety Equipment, 1991)
Rosenow, Frank, *Seagoing Knots* (W.W. Norton, New York, 1990)
Shaw, George Russell, *Knots – Useful & Ornamental* (Bonanza Books, New York, 1924 and 1933)
Spencer, Charles L., *Knots, Splices & Fancy Work* (Brown, Son & Fergusson, Glasgow, 1934)
Sweet, John, *Scout Pioneering* (Scout Association, London, 1974)
Toss, Brion, *The Rigger's Apprentice* International Marine Publishing Co, Camden, Maine, 1984)
Trower, Nola, *Knots and Ropework* (Helmsman Books, Marlborough, Wiltshire, 1992)
Vare, Alan B., *The Hardy Book of Fisherman's Knots* (Camden Publishing, London, 1987)
Warner, Charles, *A Fresh Approach to Knotting and Ropework* (Warner, Yanderra, NSW, 1992)

ACKNOWLEDGEMENTS

The author is indebted to David Ierston, marine sales manager for English Braids Ltd, who supplied superb cordage for this book.

The following, from whom the cordage was obtained to tie most of the specimen knots illustrated, were also generous with their time and advice: Brenda Risdon (Oakhurst Quality Products Ltd.); Kevin Keatley (K.J.K. Ropeworks); James Martin (Marlow Ropes Ltd.); Des & Liz Pawson (Footrope Knots).

A special extra acknowledgement is due to Des Pawson who, by allowing access to his home and workplace, made possible the unique portraits of traditional ropework that enrich this book.

ORGANIZATIONS

The International Guild of Knot Tyers was established in 1982 and now has a worldwide membership. It is a registered educational charity, dedicated to preserving and promoting the art, craft and science of knots.

Anyone – expert or novice – interested in tying knots may join. IGKT members enjoy a quarterly magazine, *Knotting Matters,* in addition to regular meetings. For more details and an application form, contact:

Nigel Harding,
IGKT Honorary Secretary,
16 Egles Grove, Uckfield, East Sussex TN22 2BY, England
Tel: 01825 760 425
e-mail:
igkt@nigelharding.demon.uk
(Knotting can also be found on the Internet.)